Joe DiMaggio

Joe

Yale UNIVERSITY PRESS

NEW HAVEN & LONDON

DiMaggio

The Long Vigil

Jerome Charyn

Published with assistance from the foundation established in memory of
Philip Hamilton McMillan of the Class of 1894, Yale College.

Lyrics from "Mrs. Robinson" copyright © 1966, Paul Simon;
used by permission of the publisher, Paul Simon Music.

Yale University Press books may be purchased in quantity for educational,
business, or promotional use. For information, please e-mail
sales.press@yale.edu (U.S. office) or sales@yaleup.co.uk (U.K. office).

Set in Janson Roman type by Newgen North America
Printed in the United States of America.

Library of Congress Cataloging-in-Publication Data
Charyn, Jerome.
Joe DiMaggio : the long vigil / Jerome Charyn.
p. cm. — (Icons of America)
Includes bibliographical references and index.
ISBN 978-0-300-12328-9 (cloth : alk. paper)
1. DiMaggio, Joe, 1914–1999. 2. Baseball players—
United States—Biography. I. Title.
GV865.D5C53 2011
796.357092—dc22
[B]   2010034294

A catalogue record for this book is available from the British Library.

This paper meets the requirements of ANSI/NISO Z39.48-1992
(Permanence of Paper).

10 9 8 7 6 5 4 3 2 1

ICONS OF AMERICA

Mark Crispin Miller, *Series Editor*

Icons of America is a series of short works written by leading scholars, critics, and writers, each of whom tells a new and innovative story about American history and culture through the lens of a single iconic individual, event, object, or cultural phenomenon.

The Hollywood Sign: Fantasy and Reality of an American Icon,
by Leo Braudy

The Big House: Image and Reality of the American Prison,
by Stephen Cox

Andy Warhol, by Arthur C. Danto

Our Hero: Superman on Earth, by Tom De Haven

Fred Astaire, by Joseph Epstein

Wall Street: America's Dream Palace, by Steve Fraser

No Such Thing as Silence: John Cage's 4'33", by Kyle Gann

Frankly, My Dear: Gone with the Wind *Revisited,* by Molly Haskell

Alger Hiss and the Battle for History, by Susan Jacoby

Nearest Thing to Heaven: The Empire State Building and American Dreams, by Mark Kingwell

Unwarranted Influence: Dwight D. Eisenhower and the Military-Industrial Complex, by James Ledbetter

The Liberty Bell, by Gary Nash

The Hamburger: A History, by Josh Ozersky

Gypsy: The Art of the Tease, by Rachel Shteir

King's Dream, by Eric J. Sundquist

Inventing a Nation: Washington, Adams, Jefferson, by Gore Vidal

Small Wonder: The Little Red Schoolhouse in History and Memory, by Jonathan Zimmerman

It is as if DiMaggio expects her to understand, with of course never a word being said, that he has not arrived at his eminence in Toots Shor's along with Hemingway and one or two select sports writers and gamblers because he is dumb or gifted or lucky but because he had an art that demanded huge concentration, and the consistent courage over the years to face into thousands of fast balls any of which could kill or cripple him if he were struck in the head.

—NORMAN MAILER, *Marilyn*

Contents

Contents

Preface

How can I ever explain the old Yankee Stadium to anyone who hasn't grown up in the Bronx? It was the one ornament we had in a borough that was nothing but a series of hinterlands. We had our exotica, such as a botanical garden and a zoo that tried (and failed) to replicate the African plains; a cemetery where Herman Melville lies; a cottage where Edgar Allan Poe might have lived; our own movie palace, the Paradise, and a few deluxe ice cream parlors; even a medley of Art Deco apartment houses on the Grand Concourse, a boulevard meant to look like the Champs-Élysées, but was only one more mirage that led nowhere, though it did skirt Yankee Stadium. And if you were lucky enough to sneak onto the roof of a building near the Concourse and 161st Street, you could gaze right into that delicious concrete bowl down the hill and catch a wide swath of green that looked like a methodical forest. During a night game (much rarer then), that deep bowl burnt with a yellow haze that belonged to the Bronx. It was our own impossible season that finished long before midnight, but seemed to linger like some endless Halloween.

Yet that was only a meager portion of its magic. The concrete bowl housed a phantom we seldom saw. His name was DiMaggio. He didn't live with the other Yankee players at *our* hotel, the Concourse Plaza, where the daughters of Bronx millionaires were married. DiMaggio lived downtown, across the Harlem River, at a Manhattan hotel. Poor as we were in '46 and '47, we still had enough gelt to get through the turnstile at Yankee Stadium and watch the phantom play. He never signed autographs, never smiled, never clowned, like outfielders on the Senators or the Indians, who would do elaborate pantomimes for us while one of their own pitchers was warming up. He didn't pretend to notice us, or fake an intimacy with the fans. He was brutal in his devotion to the game. He didn't fidget, didn't slap his glove. There was no off-time for Joltin' Joe. Even if we were behind by seven runs, and a new relief pitcher trotted in from the Yankee bullpen, he didn't waver once. He would watch that pitcher's windup, study his nervous tics, as if every gesture on the field were part of some mysterious baseball map that only he could master. He knocked the scoreboard out of our heads, and the batting averages we knew by heart. We hadn't come to preside over the fall of the Red Sox and the Browns, or to see DiMaggio hit a home run. We weren't acolytes. We were students of the game, and by studying DiMaggio as he stood there in center field, alert and alone, with his wounded heel, we came a little closer to understanding the sway that baseball had over us. It wasn't statistics or the panoply of pennant flags. It was the power to hypnotize, to fill us with a fever. This strange man showed us how serious the game was—for DiMaggio, and for ourselves, it was a matter of life and death.

The Yankee Clipper reached beyond baseball into the American psyche. He was our suffering hero, gloriously alone in center field, when play itself was a kind of sacrifice. He arrived like a lightning bolt in the middle of the Great Depression and seemed to soothe us all.

So celebrated was he during his rookie season—1936—that even President Roosevelt had come to watch him play. It was the second game of the World Series against the New York Giants; the Bronx Bombers were ahead 18–4 in the ninth inning. DiMaggio, running like a devil, made an impossible behind-the-shoulder catch in the deepest hinterland of the Polo Grounds. At that very moment FDR appeared. He was riding in his open limousine toward the gates in center field. And he waved to Joe with the brim of his hat. All of America could have been in the stands, as the crowd acknowledged that salute with what one sports writer called "a final, rippling cheer."

And now we have a new Yankee Stadium that looms right across the street from the old one, on the site of a former playground and park. You can find images of Alex Rodriguez & Co. along its outer wall. But the stadium's inner world is no longer visible from the Grand Concourse. The old stadium once sat beside it like a mournful ghost. Much of its carcass has been picked clean. But you can still catch a whiff of Joltin' Joe while it's there. You can still recall the Jolter's leaps. That carcass might even conjure up a wild era when players strove without ever really getting rich, when no one, not even DiMaggio, ever made millions wearing a Yankee uniform.

But one thing continues to plague us about our memory of the Jolter. Why did his intensity and terrifying heat in center field diminish away from the field and leave him with so little sense of purpose? Why was there such a haunting dissonance between the man and his image, or did *we* impose an image upon him that was utterly removed from the man? He seemed to fall into the land of trivia once he left the Yankees. Why couldn't his prowess as a player have kept him in good stead? Was there something corrosive for DiMaggio about the very nature of celebrity? He was one of the most idolized men in America, yet he'd become his own haunted house. While still a Yankee, beloved by half the nation, he would sit like some magnificent hermit at Toots Shor's, the Manhattan watering hole of sports stars and other nabobs. DiMaggio was the prince of Table One. No one could approach him without Toots' approval. He sat with Jackie Gleason or Frank Sinatra and Ernest Hemingway, and he never said a word all night. Did *their* celebrity shield him? Was he safe around Sinatra and "Hem"? Or was it an omen of things to come? A shyness that would cripple him once he didn't have the security of his cavern in center field? Why did he become so dysfunctional and end his days in a golden ghetto, frightened of his own fame yet needing to guard it with a stubborn, maddening will? He lived long enough to become the grand old man of baseball who could share his wisdom with his fans and younger players. What was there about the Yankee Clipper's inner torment that never allowed him to do so? Why did he disappear inside himself, like a living ghost?

Chronology

1914   Joe DiMaggio is born (November 25) in Martinez, California, a fishing village twenty-five miles north of San Francisco, the eighth child of Giuseppe and Rosalie Mercurio DiMaggio, immigrants from Isola della Femmine, a bleak island off the coast of Palermo, where Crusaders supposedly abandoned their unfaithful wives.

1915   The DiMaggios move to San Francisco's North Beach neighborhood.

1917   Dom DiMaggio, Joe's youngest brother, is born (February 12). Joe will have a lifelong rivalry with Dom, who is much cleverer outside the realm of baseball. He will have less of a rivalry with his brother Vince (born in 1912), an outfielder in the National League.

1918   Ted Williams is born (August 20) in San Diego, California, with practically a bat in his cradle; he will begin to haunt local sandlots long before he is ten.

1926   Marilyn Monroe is born (June 1) under the name Norma Jeane Mortensen in Los Angeles, the daughter of Gladys

xiii

Monroe Mortensen Baker—a woman with a myriad of husbands, lovers, and names—and a father who isn't really known but might have been Martin Edward Mortensen, a meterman whom Gladys left after four months of marriage. Gladys, who is quite unstable, will hand her two-week-old baby over to the Bolanders, a couple who care for foster children. For most of her life Marilyn will fantasize that Clark Gable was her real father.

1931   Mickey Mantle is born (August 13) in a mining town, Spavinaw, Oklahoma. His father, Mutt Mantle, will raise him to be a baseball player almost from birth.

1933   A high school dropout who doesn't want to be a fisherman like his dad, Joe leaps right from a dinky semipro club to the San Francisco Seals of the Pacific Coast League and breaks a league record by hitting safely in sixty-one consecutive games.

1936   Joe joins the Yankees and becomes perhaps the most heralded rookie who ever played in the big leagues; with Joe ensconced in center field, the Bombers will win their first pennant and World Series in four years. Right from the start he is considered the premier outfielder in the American League.

1939   After two years of courtship, Joe marries a beautiful blond showgirl from Minnesota, Dorothy Arnold, in San Francisco (November 10).

1941   Joe becomes the most celebrated athlete in America as he hits safely in fifty-six consecutive games; his son, Joe DiMaggio, Jr., is born (October 23) and is almost as celebrated as Joe himself.

1942   Joe, the hero of 1941, is plagued by all sorts of doubt as other baseball heroes have gone off to war; Dorothy prepares to file for divorce.

1943   Joe reluctantly enlists in the Army Air Force.

1946   Joe returns to baseball without a wife. He begins to be plagued by injuries. For the first time in the big leagues he will bat under .300.

1949   Casey Stengel, Joe's nemesis, is named manager of the New York Yankees.

1951   Mickey Mantle arrives at the Yankee camp with as much attention from fans and the press as Joe had first received in 1936. But Mantle will not have a great rookie season. In December, after a mediocre season of his own, Joe announces his retirement from baseball.

1952   Joe meets Marilyn Monroe; the nation is immediately drawn to this marvelous couple, even though there's a certain ambiguity about their romance. Joe wants to marry her; Marilyn is reluctant.

1954   Joe and Marilyn are married in San Francisco (January 14) while she is under suspension at Twentieth Century–Fox. They leave for a honeymoon in Japan. In October, Marilyn files for divorce.

1962   Joe remains obsessed with Marilyn, who had married and divorced playwright Arthur Miller; her own career seems on the decline. Marilyn agrees to marry Joe again but dies of an overdose of barbiturates during the evening of August 4–5.

1999   Joe DiMaggio dies in Hollywood, Florida (March 8), after having undergone surgery for lung cancer and contracting pneumonia and a lung infection. While he lay dying there was "a national vigil," according to the *New York Times.*

Joe DiMaggio

Prologue
Pinocchio in Pinstripes

I.

He was the nonpareil, missed from the moment he retired in 1951. "Where have you gone, Joe DiMaggio?" asked Paul Simon in 1967. "A nation turns its lonely eyes to you." Thus there was a lament for DiMaggio long before he died, in 1999. And when he lay ill in a hospital during the last days of his life, the flurry of reports about his condition could have been about a pontiff or a president, not a baseball player who toiled in the outfield at Yankee Stadium for thirteen years. DiMaggio seemed to override baseball and sports itself. He was the lonely practitioner of some lost American art—America's one and only prince, who happened to have been a baseball player.

Babe Ruth was loved; Ty Cobb was reviled. Joe DiMaggio was revered, looked upon with an almost religious awe. He was the first saint of baseball when baseball itself was a religion, an icon of American life, "the binding national myth," according to David Halberstam in *Summer of '49;* and even as reverberations began to grow about his tie to gangsters and gamblers, his disregard for his only son, his mauling of Marilyn Monroe (he bruised her face and might have broken her thumb), DiMaggio still managed to survive as *our* troubadour.

As Marilyn's own aura multiplies year after year, and we see her now as a great comic artist, much more complex than most of the men who hovered around her—Arthur Miller, Elia Kazan, Yves Montand, Frank Sinatra, and both Kennedy boys—Marilyn and Joe have become America's mythic couple, with a troubled friendship and romance that was more constant than any marriage, even their own. Whatever his faults, he was the only man worthy of her, who did not *use* Marilyn or feed off her fame, as Miller and Montand did. When she was trapped inside a madhouse in 1961, it was DiMaggio who got her out, threatening to tear down the place, "piece of wood by piece of wood," if it did not produce her in five minutes. When she lay about like some besotted prisoner in Frank Sinatra's Palm Springs compound, it was DiMaggio who stood outside the gate, keeping his own vigil, just as he kept vigil in the caverns of Yankee Stadium.[1]

He was always keeping vigil, and that's why we remember him. His greatness has less to do with statistics than with his *devotion* to baseball, or to anything he cared about. He had a purity and a natural grace that few others had. He was, as Grantland Rice reminds us in "An Ode to the Jolter," a "drifting phantom" with "movement none could match." Ted Williams, his one great rival, was utterly bored in the outfield. "There were tales of his conduct in the outfield, where he'd sit down between batters or practice swinging an imaginary bat, watching his leg-stride, watching his wrist-break, watching everything except balls hit to him," wrote Richard Ben Cramer.[2]

It was Cramer's biography of the Yankee Clipper, published in 2000, that seemed to deflate DiMaggio, to tarnish him for the twenty-first century. Subtitled *The Hero's Life*, it attacks the "hero machine" that helped create DiMaggio and reveals a man who didn't want to go to war, who was utterly friendless except for a coterie of sycophants, who stalked Marilyn after their divorce, who sold his World Series rings to pay for his lodging, and who never spent an instant marveling "at the beauty of anything. Except maybe a broad."[3]

Cramer's book is itself a marvel that digs deep into the DiMaggio myth as it unmans him piece by piece. But its picture of the Jolter is far too reductive and bleak. DiMaggio was much more than the blind apparatus of a machine that spat out heroes and ruined them in the process. He wasn't as calculating as Cramer loves to think. He was like an idiot savant whose magic was born on a baseball field and abandoned him once he left it.

No one, not even Cramer, doubted him in center field. "It was a special place—not just the vastness in the Bronx, but every center field: the largest suzerainty in the game's realm, it had to be patrolled by a prince."[4]

DiMaggio was that prince, alone in his suzerainty, unrivaled, a hunter waiting for his prey. DiMaggio land was not simply center field but right-center and left-center, so that the other two outfielders were appendages who didn't dare enter his territory unless the prince gave them permission to do so. "He was a world by himself," recalls Henry Kissinger, who first saw DiMaggio patrol the outfield from a seat in the bleachers in 1938, when Kissinger was a German Jewish refugee living with his parents in Washington Heights. "There was nobody who could take over a ballpark like he could."[5]

And Kissinger wasn't an exceptional witness: so much of DiMaggio's almost magical fame comes from his own fans, from those he marked for life, whether it be Ernest Hemingway, who wrote about "the great DiMaggio" in *The Old Man and the Sea*, a sports writer such as Jimmy Cannon, a social critic such as David Halberstam, a literary critic such as Christopher Lehmann-Haupt, the biologist and baseball aficionado Stephen Jay Gould, or the rest of us, who were astonished by what we saw, and were able to find a language to tell others about it, to describe DiMaggio's own language, his economy of motion, his lyricism as he roamed center field. There was a kind of heartbreak, as we worried that he might disappear in that enormous expanse of space, that no one man could withstand all the wind, not even the Yankee Clipper, that the leaping gazelle we saw was some aberration, a phantom put there by our own wish to create some creature more perfect than ourselves. No fellow human being could possibly look that good, but DiMaggio did.

2.

He wasn't good-looking in a conventional way. He had a pointy nose, like Pinocchio, and a terrible overbite. He had the face of a handsome horse. When he first began to play for the San Francisco Seals in 1933, he was burdened by two buckteeth. One of the scouting reports called him "a gawky, awkward kid, all arms and legs like a colt, and inclined to be surly." But the awkwardness went away, and it was the colt that remained, that incredible sense of a constant, dancing motion. Still, he wasn't coltish off the field. He had little social grace. He never smiled and couldn't banter with his teammates. He seemed frightened of language. He had no real education to speak of outside baseball itself. The son of Italian immigrants who had never mastered English, he left high school after one year, worked on the docks, and played a little baseball. Unlike Ted Williams, a beanpole who lived only to hit a ball, DiMaggio fell into a career, followed his older brother Vince to the Seals, and quickly took his place on the team. It wasn't out of arrogance or some cruel calculation: it was that absolute sense of his own gift.

"On the ball field I was never uncertain. I knew what I was doing out there."[6]

In 1933 the Seals were all the baseball San Franciscans could see, since the major leagues reached no farther west than St. Louis, with the Browns and the Cardinals; and the Seal team, managed by former Dodger and Phillie batting champion Lefty O'Doul, was like a major league all of its own, with a mountain of fans and sportswriters. By the end of his first season with the Seals, DiMaggio was already a minor myth, with a sixty-one-game hitting streak. The Seals had never had a player like DiMaggio. "I wanted to be the greatest I could be. I burned in my belly to be the best there was."[7]

And he played with this intensity, with this fierce will, throughout his career. Ted Williams also "burned in the belly," but with Williams it was more of an abstract ideal, a search for perfection that often did not include teammates or the fans. Even John Updike, Williams' greatest fan, had to admit: "Seeking a perfectionist's vacuum, he has quixotically desired to sever the game from the ground of paid spectatorship and publicity that supports it."[8]

But DiMaggio was never quixotic as a player, never lost inside his own cocoon; the perfection he sought was within the *immediate* parameters of a game, with all its smells, its cries, and the hurly-burly of the moment. He played to win and wore himself out trying to win. There were other ballplayers who were just as complete, but almost none who had that moment-to-moment concentration and control, as if he were connected by some invisible string to every other position, every base, from his outpost in center field.

"You saw him standing out there and you knew you had a pretty damn good chance to win the baseball game," recalled Yankee pitcher Red Ruffing. Outfielder Tommy Henrich recognized how much DiMaggio gave of himself with every single play, so that his presence alone created "a considerable edge." Perhaps the greatest treat of DiMaggio's era were his duels with Bob Feller, the

Cleveland Indian ace, whose fastball and wicked curve were almost as mythic as the Yankee Clipper. Feller arrived the same season DiMaggio did, in 1936, a seventeen-year-old farm boy from Iowa who struck out fifteen batters in his very first game and was soon baseball's preeminent pitcher. According to Cleveland catcher Jim Hegan, who crouched right behind the Clipper during many of these duels, "Feller had a great deal of emotion and excitement about him when he was facing DiMaggio. DiMaggio never showed any of that against Feller. You couldn't tell if he was facing Feller or . . . some kid up from the minors five minutes ago."[9]

But Yankee outfielder Charlie Keller captures a very different DiMaggio during these duels. "You could actually see the veins and muscles in DiMaggio's neck stand out," Keller recalled to David Halberstam. "They were like red cords. His whole body was tensed." Thus DiMaggio himself was a curious contradiction, a man whose play seemed effortless while he *suffered* on the field, his expression often "as sad and haunted as a matador's," according to Gay Talese. He was, to his worshipful fans, "long and lean, like a holy man in an El Greco painting," writes George Vecsey of the *New York Times*.[10]

If DiMaggio looked haunted, it's because he played like a haunted man, a hunger artist who was utterly spent after a game. "He always gave so much of himself on the field that there wasn't much left when the game was over," recalls Yankee pitcher Ed Lopat. And stories began to abound about his life off the field, where he was as much of a mystery. A month after the 1936 season began, DiMaggio was mobbed wherever he went and could not leave Yankee Stadium without a phalanx of policemen and security guards to protect him from the fans. "I think DiMaggio was the loneliest man I ever knew," according to Lopat. "He couldn't even eat a meal in a hotel restaurant. The fans wouldn't let him. He led the league in room service."[11]

He would visit the best whorehouses in Manhattan, where he could prowl behind locked doors, but he had to eschew satin sheets because "his knees kept slipping." Eventually he would find a few watering holes where he could sit at a select table and not be seen. He could not shake his own shyness. He almost never spoke. He preferred to hide in some corner and read comic books—a little later he would fall in love with Superman. His sudden, almost violent fame, which had pulled him right out of obscurity, must have made him feel akin to a comic book hero with supernatural powers.[12]

Once he left baseball, he became "a legend without a purpose," a sleek Pinocchio in expensive suits, obsessed with the way he looked, but with no real imagination and little to do. He was a television commentator who could not even repeat his own name without looking at a prompter. A lack of education had left him stranded, distrustful, frightened of other people, a man without curiosity.[13]

Enter Marilyn Monroe. She met him on a "blind date" in the spring of 1952. Marilyn's career was about to crash-dive. The nude calendar she had posed for in 1949 had suddenly surfaced: there was not a single starlet who had posed in the nude and survived. And so her mentor, Hollywood columnist Sidney Skolsky, hit upon a plan to save her career: Joe DiMaggio, the retired prince of baseball and the nearest thing to royalty America had ever had. The commotion surrounding her dates with DiMaggio smothered all the flak over the nudie calendar. And there he was: Pinocchio *and* Prince Charming.

They were both childlike in their cultural void, a void with a great deal of sexual heat; yet that was not enough to bind them. Marilyn wanted to crawl outside her narrowness, and DiMaggio did not. He preferred to sit at home and eat dinner off a tray while watching Westerns on TV. All his adventure, all his shrewdness, had been on a playing field, and he had no more caverns to race across, no more balls to catch, no more duels with Bob Feller.

7

Nothing in his background of a fisherman's family had prepared him for the whirlwind of Marilyn Monroe. "She's a plain kid," he told Jimmy Cannon. "She'd give up the business if I asked her. She'd quit the movies in a minute. It means nothing to her."[14]

He'd looked into her eyes and seen a mirror of himself, as if she did not exist outside his want and his will, while she danced around him with her own ambition. He'd never understand how bright she was, how much more subtle than he would ever be. "I'm not interested in money," she said in the very last interview she gave. "I just want to be wonderful." DiMaggio's life had become all about money and the things it could measure, whether it was the mink coat he bought for Marilyn, his worth as a baseball player, or the price of every baseball he signed at memorabilia shows.[15]

Norman Mailer is the one who best understood Marilyn's dilemma as Mrs. Joe DiMaggio: "She has to be suffering all the anguish of living with a man who will save her in a shipwreck or learn to drive a dog team to the North Pole (if her plane should crash there) but sits around the apartment watching television all night," and "wishes to end her movie career!"[16]

But when she dumps DiMaggio after 274 days of marriage, she forgets how prone to shipwrecks she really is, how the storm center of her own energy leaves her in a constant state of chaos: it's DiMaggio who will get her out of the madhouse, DiMaggio who will bury her, who will clean up all the mess, who will have roses sent to her crypt *religiously* for twenty years. "Rain or shine those flowers [were] delivered." She will haunt him for the rest of his life. She was the one woman who was larger than his own calculations, who shook him out of his shell. When he brought her to his watering hole, Toots Shor's, the most misogynistic bar in Manhattan, where husbands were not supposed to bring their wives more than once or twice, "the place went electric," hummed with Marilyn's own electric life, so that for a moment he wasn't some sad-faced matador, that sufferer on and off the field, that man of measurements. But it did not last long. Without Marilyn he went from the Yankee Clipper to Mr. Coffee, who could measure our lives in coffee spoons, and the king of memorabilia shows, whose life was limited to the signatures he sold.[17]

On the day I began writing this book (July 17, 2007) there was an article in the *New York Times* entitled "Hard to Figure: The Drab Legacy of Jottin' Joe." It seems that the Clipper had kept a "journal" of his daily activities from 1982 to 1993: twenty-four hundred pages bound in twenty-nine folders to be sold by Steiner Sports, a Westchester company that trades in memorabilia. Steiner Sports called this treasure trove a marvelous means for DiMaggio to "convey his feelings and emotions." But it is rather a testimony to the sadness and the loneliness of an idiot savant. His scribbles are filled with the details of a demented man, with jottings about when he woke up, if and when he took a steam bath, his negotiations with Mr. Coffee.

The one fleck of emotion seems to come from all the celebrations in 1991 honoring the fiftieth anniversary of his fifty-six-game hitting streak that "immortalized" him as the most famous man in America. He's bothered by the brouhaha and intrusions upon his privacy. And he says with a certain pique that had he known beforehand about all this fuss, he would have ended his streak "after 40 games."

There's not one mention of Marilyn, only the trivia of signing baseballs, as if he had no interior life. And then we realize what is lacking. He isn't senile. He is a man who had no language outside the lyricism of his own body. He danced for us on a playing field with a terrifying power, in spite of the bone spurs in his heel. Part of this fire came from the deep insecurity of a man who had a fear of words. Marilyn had much the same fear. She would freeze in front of a camera whenever she had to mouth a few lines.

While making *Some Like It Hot* (1959), Billy Wilder had to tape the simplest bit of dialogue to the nearest prop if he wanted her to say her lines. But she hypnotizes us as Sugar Kane, the warbler in an all-girls band. Just as she hypnotized Joe, held him in a trance. She was the one person on the planet who seemed to wake him up, to rouse his mind and his emotions. It was a brittle romance with many interruptions, but still a love story we can't seem to forget, between the mute man whose glory came while he pranced around in pinstripes on an endless field and the finest, funniest actress of the fifties, who was dismissed in her own time as a freak and a sad case.

Joe's jottings are the ravaged songs of a troubadour, the ravings of a man who fell into trivia while he mourned Marilyn in some part of him he did not care to show. The signings were subterfuge. He never lost that exquisite edge he had on the field to lock out unimportant details. He cloaked himself in memorabilia shows, the minutia of signing bats and balls, wore the disguise of Mr. Coffee. He burned in his belly until the very end, but would share it with us only for a little while, on the playing field, where his galloping and the wonderful whip of his bat revealed his pride and his love of the game and never intruded upon this most private of men.

We remember him now as an icon out of our own rumbling past. It's not his hitting streak that haunts us, but what that streak represents—his fierce concentration, his fierce will. Gay Talese wasn't wrong to compare him to a matador. There are no bulls on a baseball diamond, yet there might as well have been. DiMaggio lived in that constant danger zone where a bull might gore a man. He took us with him into that realm of the absolute. It was a ride we would never forget.

3.

Perhaps no one understood the Clipper as well or worshiped him as much as Toots Shor. Born in South Philadelphia in 1903, Bernard

"Toots" Shor grew up in a tough Irish neighborhood and learned to protect his own little territory. His roughhousing would hold him in good stead when he became a bouncer and doorman at several Manhattan speakeasies, including the Five O'Clock Club, a mob front on West 54th. He was "the only Jew kid" who ever worked for mobster Owney Madden. Shor was six feet two and had the shoulders of a football player. He also had the ability to make and keep good friends. It was at the Five O'Clock Club where he first met James Cagney and George Raft and where the boisterous myth of Toots began. "If he doesn't insult you, he doesn't love you, and if he doesn't love you, you have missed a chunk of life," said one of Toots' coterie, actor Pat O'Brien.[18]

The Five O'Clock Club morphed into a restaurant and saloon that opened in 1940 on West 51st Street. Nothing was ever the same after that. It was where boxers, baseball players, and sportswriters ruled rather than presidents, politicians, and other kingpins, though Harry Truman and J. Edgar Hoover were always welcome at Toots Shor's, along with mobster Frank Costello, who may have owned a piece of the saloon. Toots adored the New York Giants, even while they hobbled around in last place, but he had one hero—Joe D. It was like a love affair between a loudmouth and a lonesome, silent center fielder. Joe called Toots every day while he was on the road, and when the Yankees were in town, he would often go directly from his perch in center field to "51 West 51." DiMaggio lived there, ate there, and learned to deal with his shyness at Table One. He belonged to Toots' little gang of "solid-gold crumb bums." Toots prized "palship" over everything else. There were "civilians" who ate and drank at his saloon from time to time, but his "crumb bums" had to be there every day. If they happened to be out of town, Toots would cry into the phone: "I miss you. Come on home. I love ya, ya creepy bum!" And he missed DiMaggio most of all.[19]

DiMaggio may have been a skinflint who expected others to pay for the pleasure of his company, but he wasn't a skinflint at Toots' saloon. He never balked when Toots donated cash to some charity in his name. He was loyal to Toots' clubhouse with its circular bar, and he was loyal to Toots. It didn't matter how often Yankee president Larry MacPhail feuded with Toots. If MacPhail wanted to have dinner with DiMaggio, it had to be at the clubhouse. Joe wouldn't meet him at the Colony or "21."

Toots' gang had to have "class," which Toots himself defined. "Class is a thing where a guy does everything decent."[20] But this was a subterfuge. Almost all of Toots' crumb bums, including DiMaggio, had a dread of anything "high-tony"—Toots' sense of character or class was a workingman's dream. Most of his pals, from Owney Madden to Jackie Gleason and George Raft, had their own private chivalry and primitive code; they were knights of the lower depths, men who had not been born into privilege and who prized loyalty above all other things.

Toots loved to say that "a saloonkeeper in the city is like a minister in a small town."[21] For his devotees, Toots' saloon had a small town's convivial lines and rules, and within this narrow world, DiMaggio was a godlike champion with the greatest class of all. He never made one phony gesture on the field, never showboated, or got into rhubarbs with other players. Toots could be a bit sentimental about Joe. "You have given me more thrills than all the rest of the champions put together. You are the biggest guy I know and the biggest thing about you is your heart." But Shor was a keen observer behind his sloppy, sentimental mask. He attended every home game, saw the dreamlike moves of a man on fire, that stillness as DiMaggio woke with the sound of a bat and seemed to burn himself alive galloping after the ball. DiMaggio didn't carouse after a game. He returned to Toots Shor's, where all the solid-gold bums had their home base.[22]

DiMaggio would guard that base through war and the strife of his first marriage. "I ain't braggin'," Toots would say, "but I think I got the best joint in New York, and to me New York is America." But not even Toots could withstand the whirlwind of Marilyn Monroe.[23]

PART I

The Player

ONE

"Our National Exaggeration"

I.

First there was Babe Ruth. No one man has ever altered a sport, changed it forever, the way Ruth did. Ruth didn't invent the home run. He simply turned it into a lethal weapon. Baseball had once been a game of wits, where pitchers and fielders dueled among themselves, and a bunt single or a base on balls could be the difference between life and death. Like parsimonious squirrels, a team would guard and nurse a one-run lead that most often would win a game. There was a constant panorama of hit-and-run plays. The home run seldom figured in this firmament. When Ruth was a nineteen-year-old rookie pitcher for the Boston Red Sox in 1914, his team hit a total of 18 home runs.

But the Red Sox soon discovered that they had a power hitter on their hands. In 1915 their young left-hander had 18 victories and led the team in home runs (4). But this wasn't the barrel-chested Ruth we like to remember. He was as long and lean as a knife, even with his broad, flaring nostrils. By 1918 he was only a part-time pitcher.

He appeared in 95 games and led the major leagues in home runs (11). In the greatest baseball blunder of all time, the cash-starved Red Sox sold their star outfielder-pitcher to the New York Yankees near the end of 1919.

Nothing was the same after that. Ruth not only hit 54 home runs in 1920, he also stole more bases than any other Yankee (14). He was a colossus nurtured in the hit-and-run era who now originated an era of his own. He packed the Polo Grounds, where the Yankees played as tenants of the New York Giants because they didn't have their own ballpark. Until Ruth arrived, the Giants and their manager, John "Muggsy" McGraw, had been the kings of Manhattan. Muggsy fought with his players, fought with umpires, fought with the fans, and had turned the Giants into baseball's most feared enterprise. They had won the second World Series, in 1905, and were featured in the Ziegfeld Follies, where statuesque blondes ran around in baseball caps and chased their rivals off the runway. But they had no rivals.

All of a sudden they had an enemy in their own house. Ruth could fill a ballpark wherever he went. Soon the National League began to suffer because it did not have a Babe of its own. The Giants were so jealous of Ruth and the fans he brought to the Polo Grounds that they kicked the Yankees out, and Colonel Jacob Ruppert, the heir to a brewery fortune and principal owner of the Yankees, was forced to build his own stadium across the Harlem River in the Bronx. Thus the Bronx Bombers were born in 1923 at Yankee Stadium, Ruth's own arena.

The Bombers won their very first World Series that year, beating the Giants 4 games to 2, with Ruth hitting 3 home runs. Ruth not only murdered McGraw, he made the Yankees rich and helped begin a dynasty. The Yankees would become the most successful franchise in baseball, going on to win 39 more pennants and 26 more World Series (and counting). It couldn't have happened without the Babe.

He dominated *all* of baseball. He turned the Yankees into a kind of public spectacle. You loved or hated the Yankees as much as you loved or hated Ruth. Fans were never indifferent to him. He wouldn't have allowed them to be—the Babe was having too much fun. Heckle him and he would climb on top of the dugout and challenge the crowds; hurl a bottle at him and he would chase the bottle-thrower into the stands; the first time he moved from the pitcher's mound to left field he began to sulk. "Gee, it's lonesome in the outfield. It's hard to keep awake with nothing to do."[1]

He reveled in every moment, had to be seen, had to be felt. He loved to mingle, to drive down Broadway in his maroon sports car or lounge in front of a hotel, "his broad nostrils sniffing at the promise of the night." He had his own vaudeville act one season, would banter and croon in his great baritone voice, but he was as much of a vaudevillian right on the field. Baseball had become his very own big show. He had, according to another player, "the prettiest swing of all," and was most pretty when he struck out, with his own kind of high drama. "In Charleston he swung so hard striking out that as he spun around, his spikes caught in the hard clay of the batter's box and wrenched an ankle. . . . No one in Carolina could recall seeing a man swing so hard he hurt himself when he missed."[2]

A new apparatus of sports writers had been built around the Babe; writing about his exploits on and off the field had created a new fabric, a new skin, out of a straggler's game that had once belonged to bumpkins. None of these bumpkins could compete with the Babe, a "country boy" from Baltimore who was raised in an orphanage even though he wasn't an orphan, the beloved bad boy of baseball who would do anything for a laugh. "He ate a hat once," according to teammate Joe Dugan. "He did. A straw hat. Took a bite out of it and ate it."[3]

But the Babe wasn't as uncontrolled as he seemed. A superb showman and manager of his own image, he hired a publicist, Christy

Walsh, and was shrewd enough to license "his name and face to sell everything from candy bars to automobiles."[4]

He was just as foxy with sports writers, could play them as seriously as he could swing into a pitch. "The man was a boy, simple, artless, genuine and unabashed," wrote Red Smith in the *New York Times.* But there was a lot of art in his artlessness. He loved to parade around with Yankee batboy Eddie Bennett, a hunchback who was the Babe's personal mascot. Bennett would run after the Babe with cups of bicarbonate of soda to fight off the heartburn that accompanied his constant quota of hot dogs. Bennett might stand over a visiting team's dugout and taunt the players while the Babe saluted them with his cup. His whole life was about performance, whether it was on the field, at a luncheon stand, or inside a bordello. "He was the noisiest fucker in North America," recalled one of his friends.[5]

It was noise itself that catapulted him, noise that got him noticed, noise that was his engine. Louder and larger than anyone else, he hit the longest home runs, created headlines for the Yankees and himself, until baseball was a kind of circus that traveled with him from town to town. Presidential candidates had to beg for the opportunity to shake his hand. He wouldn't pose with Herbert Hoover in 1928. "Tell him I'll be glad to talk to him if he wants to meet me under the stands," he told his reporter friends, who followed the Babe and all his exploits, fed off his furor, and were a crucial part of his endless circus train. "Without the Babe there wasn't an awful lot to write about," said Dan Daniel of the *World-Telegram,* who jealously guarded his access to the Babe until no one else at the *Telegram* was allowed to go near him without Daniel's permission.[6]

Daniel and other sports writers such as Grantland Rice helped establish a "baseball nation" around Ruth. And that little nation was severely rocked when the Yanks got rid of Ruth after the 1934 season. The Babe was thirty-nine years old. He joined the Boston Braves, was hyped as the new sultan of the National League, but couldn't even finish out 1935. He quit after socking 6 home runs in 28 games, striking out 26 times, and with a batting average way below .200. He had become a jester and clown; dubbed vice president of the Braves, he made no decisions at all, on the field or off. The Dodgers would hire him as a coach in 1938; but again he had nothing to do. "He was like an ex-President, famous but useless," according to his biographer Robert Creamer.[7]

He went hunting, he bowled, he fished, and he waited and waited, "but the call to manage never came." Owners didn't want this unmanageable man to manage their teams. He was reckless in their eyes, irresponsible. He couldn't be bullied. He was much too large for any of their domains. He continued to bowl and began to waste away with throat cancer. "The famous round face had become so hollowed out that his snub nose looked long," Murray Schumach wrote in the *New York Times*. His hair had gone all white.[8]

"The termites have got me," Ruth told Connie Mack, owner-manager of the Philadelphia Athletics, just before he died in 1948.[9]

2.

How are we to measure such a man when the truth is that he was unmeasurable? We can't find him in the records he broke, in his slugging percentage, in his bases on balls. God knows the games he might have won had he remained a pitcher for the Red Sox and hit only an occasional home run. He was far more valuable when he was their ace left-hander. They won three pennants with Ruth on the mound. But what if he had never been sold to the Yankees? Would he have seized our imagination in the same way?

It's hard to tell. The myth of Ruth was born and nurtured in Manhattan. New York, according to F. Scott Fitzgerald, "had all the iridescence of the beginning of the world." Ruth became part of

Fitzgerald's Jazz Age. And the heart of the Jazz Age was Manhattan, which would introduce "a new kind of culture—mass culture—and a new kind of city—a city of desires and dreams." The Babe fell right into this city of desires, even though Yankee Stadium itself was in the grasslands of the Bronx. When he arrived in Manhattan, Ruth lived right on Broadway, at the Ansonia; a Beaux-Arts palace built in 1904, it quickly became the home and hangout of actors, opera singers, musicians, and Broadway impresarios. Ruth was its first and only baseball player. He would drop baseballs down its winding stairwell and practice his swing on the landings. He would drive down Broadway in a coonskin coat, visit jazz clubs with Bix Beiderbecke, and haunt Manhattan's nightlife. Ezra Pound had been mesmerized by this same electric life. New York, with its panorama of electric signs, made "the seeing of visions superfluous. . . . Squares upon squares of flames, set and cut into one another. Here is our poetry, for we have pulled down the stars to our will."[10]

And Ruth himself had some of the same electric flare in a city where public relations bled right into the culture. He was "the first sports figure in history to be packaged like a product," as he licensed himself, like some human billboard that towered over Broadway.[11]

He was "our national exaggeration," an outsized creature who stood alone. There was a sense of danger about him. He'd exploded onto the landscape with his "restless, roving energy," and neither baseball nor the country was ever the same. One might even say that he pulled baseball into the Jazz Age. The crowds that followed him everywhere—the sycophants, the sports writers, the fans— loved to see him clown. But they wanted much, much more than that. They wanted to live near that sense of danger, to feel the high drama that he could add to a game, destroying a team with one or two deadly swats of his bat, so that when he hit his 60th home run on September 30, 1927, in a game against the Washington Senators, the sports writers would declare "Ruth 4, Senators 2."[12]

That was Ruth's real legacy. He was the Sultan of Swat, the magician of the long ball whose tape-measure home runs soon became a kind of national hunger, an addiction that latched onto baseball and never let go.

TWO

The Walloping Wop

I.

Enter DiMaggio.

It's 1936, and he's a star before he ever swings a bat at Yankee Stadium. It's on account of the Babe, whose aura still clung to the playing field. According to Yankee outfielder George Selkirk, "We needed a leader after Ruth left. Gehrig wasn't a leader. He was just a good old plowhorse."[1]

Ruth's disappearance from the Bronx seemed to signal the end of a dynasty and the Yankees' grip on the American League. There was an emptiness, a terrible void, that no one could fill. It didn't matter that the Giants had Carl Hubbell, the left-handed ace of the National League; the Giants were part of another nation that had never had Babe Ruth.

And behold! There was a rookie from the Seals that everyone was writing about: "Fans Expect Recruit from Coast to be Cobb, Ruth, Jackson in One," said the *Sporting News*. DiMaggio had neither the wit nor the bluster of Babe Ruth. But the Yankees needed an heir apparent. His arrival was nothing less than marvelous.[2]

What made him different was that he didn't have the usual rookie shivers. It was as if he had been born in the major leagues. "The pitchers couldn't intimidate him," recalled Hank Greenberg, Detroit's great slugger. "They threw at his head a lot, especially when he broke in. He would just move his head back out of the way of the pitch and never move his body. He'd never say anything. He'd never make a face; he'd never let the pitcher know it bothered him one single bit. He was absolutely fearless."[3]

He fell into a slump near the end of May, but fans and sports writers continued to love him. Ruth had given birth to the "baseball nation" of sports writers, and when the Yankees banished him to the Boston Braves, the writers of that nation were incredibly listless; most were in New York, with the Yankees their private territory and privileged beat. And had the contours of Ruth's greatness not been there, his outsized proportions that loomed over the game and seemed to dwarf everyone else, we would never have had such "Lavish Newspaper Ballyhoo."[4]

The hysteria was already there, that need to find another almost fictive character in a Yankee uniform. The fans didn't want a *second* Babe Ruth but someone who would rid them of their loneliness for the Babe. And they chose this buck-toothed boy.

2.

"He understood the power of silence," wrote Paul Simon, silence in every sense.[5] He didn't have the Babe's corkscrew swing, that complete twist of his body every time he struck out, so that the fans suffered with him. DiMaggio seldom struck out. And there would be a peculiar hush every time he came near the batter's box; the fans could feel his concentration and did not want to violate it. When he moved to center field by the middle of the season (after

colliding with Yankee center fielder Myril Hoag and sending him
to the hospital), their devotion was complete: DiMaggio was all by
himself in that immense prairie, and when he galloped he galloped
for them.

Even the sports writers were stunned: he'd sprung whole out of
some magic box, like no other rookie they had ever seen. He was
on the cover of *Time* magazine, got more votes than any other outfielder on the American League All-Star team, and was the first
rookie ever to play as an All-Star, though he bobbled the ball and
lost the game for the American League. Win or lose, DiMaggio got
all the attention.

And the Yankees were winning with Joe DiMaggio; they pulled
ahead of the poor second-place Tigers by 19 games, and beat the
Giants in the World Series 4 games to 2, thus beginning a second
Yankee dynasty, as potent as the first. During DiMaggio's thirteen years at the Stadium, the Yankees would "seize" ten pennants
and nine World Series. There were other stars, some with greater
seasons than his own, but it was DiMaggio's team even when Joe
Gordon, Phil Rizzuto, or Yogi Berra was Most Valuable Player and
the Yankee Clipper hobbled around for half the year.

But 1936 was all his own, even if Gehrig was the real powerhouse,
with 49 home runs to DiMaggio's 29. Fans were insatiable when it
came to Joe; tales about the games were just not enough. They had
to read his autobiography in the *World-Telegram*, with Dan Daniel
as ghostwriter. And so the saga began of the Italian fisherman's boy,
with eight brothers and sisters, born near San Francisco in 1914;
the son of a Sicilian who found the American way, who breathed
baseball, teaching himself to bat with a broken oar. But in all the
stories about him two things were stressed: his Italian background
and his absolute love of baseball. It was an era of immigrants, with
large Italian populations in every city where DiMaggio played; New
York alone had over a million men, women, and children of Italian

heritage in 1936, 17 percent of the population. Mention of Di-Maggio as "the Italian lad" or "the Walloping Wop" wasn't simply a crass appeal by the Yankee management to lure Italian-Americans through the turnstiles. It was a kind of credo, a revelation that baseball had grown up and was no longer exclusively for rednecks and country boys; if black Americans remained invisible in the major leagues (they sat in segregated bleacher seats in St. Louis) and could rarely be found at Yankee Stadium or Fenway Park, Italians and Jews, at least, had their players and fans: Detroit had Hank Greenberg, a rival to Babe Ruth; and the Bombers had their own Italian contingent, second baseman Tony Lazzeri, shortstop Frankie Crosetti, and DiMaggio, all three refugees from San Francisco.

America was still a white Protestant world, and there was often a subtle prejudice against DiMaggio himself. In a May 1, 1939, cover story about DiMaggio in *Life* magazine, author Noel Busch wrote: "Although he learned Italian first, Joe, now twenty-four, speaks English without an accent and is otherwise well adapted to most United States mores. Instead of olive oil or smelly grease, he keeps his hair slick with water. He never reeks of garlic and prefers chicken chow mein to spaghetti."[6]

3.

He would have six glorious years from 1936 to 1941, when he was the premier ballplayer in the land. He won Most Valuable Player awards twice, in 1939 and 1941, and should have won in 1937, his very best year in baseball, when he hit 46 home runs (the most in the majors), drove in 167 runs (second only to Greenberg), and batted .346 (third in the league), scored the most runs, 151, and had the highest slugging average, .673. He was twenty-two years old. He won the batting title in 1939, hitting over .400 until he was hampered by an eye allergy in September and finished at .381. That year the Red Sox would unleash the Kid, Ted Williams, their own twenty-year-old sensation, the first rookie ever to lead the league in runs batted in. The Kid had also come out of some magic box. Born in San Diego in 1918, he was four years younger than DiMaggio and longed to be the greatest hitter there ever was. He couldn't stand in front of a mirror without pretending to swing a bat, or go to the movies without squeezing a rubber ball to strengthen his grip. He batted .406 in 1941, but he still couldn't steal DiMaggio's thunder.

The Clipper wasn't being *too* unfair when he said that the Kid "throws like a broad, and he runs like a ruptured duck." Williams did have a feeble throwing arm, and he did look funny chasing fly balls. But he could also have been DiMaggio's phantom brother. He too was a loner, a secretive man who lived at a hotel rather than have a real address, and who was quick to anger. But Williams couldn't control his rage, and DiMaggio did. Williams would spit at the fans who heckled him, wouldn't tip his hat after he hit a home run. His father was a photographer in San Diego, his mother a religious woman "with a will of steel who gave her life to the Salvation Army" and often neglected him. And he became a wanderer in his own home, and would remain a wanderer, with baseball as his only fixture. He rarely drank anything harder than malted milk. But the farther he ran from his mother, the closer he seemed to get: he had his own will of steel, with baseball as his religion. If she was "the Angel of Tijuana," who crossed the border to save people's souls, he was the secret angel of Fenway Park, fighting the demons of baseball—fans, managers, owners, sports writers—to save his own soul and secure his fame.[7]

DiMaggio had other demons. He was even more secretive than the Kid, with only the language of baseball to soothe him, as if he were hiding in center field in plain sight of fifty thousand fans. "I guess I know Joe almost forty years now," Hank Greenberg would tell Maury Allen in 1975, long after he and DiMaggio had retired.

"We've played hundreds of games against each other. I've talked to him hundreds of times at banquets and at [Toots] Shor's and places like that. In a way, though, I guess I don't really know him. I don't know if anybody knows Joe DiMaggio."[8]

It is this strange aura that separates DiMaggio from Williams or Greenberg or any other player. Williams could be read, and DiMaggio couldn't. Williams was knowable, reachable, in a way that DiMaggio wasn't. We can understand Williams' passion and his *strangeness*. He wants us to marvel at him but not to interfere with his pursuit for perfection at the plate. DiMaggio never lived in such an abstract realm. He was almost autistic. He's locked inside himself even while he runs like an antelope. No one could really discern him in center field. His gods and demons were utterly his own.

But nothing seemed to hurt him in those golden years before World War II, not his injuries, not his demons. Fans heckled him for the first time in 1938, when he had a salary dispute with the Yankee management and missed spring training and the first twelve games. It startled DiMaggio to hear all that booing, but he never spat at the fans and he still tipped his hat after hitting a home run. He just crawled deeper inside himself and revealed even less than before. "I woke up in the middle of the night hearing the boos. I got up, smoked a cigarette, and walked the floor. You keep saying you will get used to it, but you never do. I stuffed my ears with cotton, but nothing helped."[9]

He became a nighthawk, spending his time at the Stork Club and "21," or at Toots Shor's when it opened in 1940; he would become Shor's most celebrated customer and client, sitting at Table One, with Shor as a benevolent bulldog who would steer other celebrities to DiMaggio's table and keep everyone else at bay.

Shy as he was, he preferred to have a shill around when he was prowling after women. "Ah," he told reporter Lou Effrat, "you know me, until midnight with girls I'm speechless." He began to romance a beautiful blond showgirl from Minnesota, Dorothy Arnold, née Dorothy Arnoldine Olsen, and married her in 1939 at the end of the playing season. But that didn't stop his prowling. Years later, after Marilyn Monroe and Dorothy Arnold were both dead, he would say with a certain wistfulness: "You know, everyone talks about how beautiful Marilyn Monroe was, and she was, but people don't remember my first wife, Dorothy Arnold. She was just as beautiful. I used to run around a lot when I was married to her. I was crazy, fucking around."[10]

But he was riding on that curious and fickle flush of his own fame, and it grew higher and higher until it burst in 1941, and he found himself the most famous man in America: the country adored everything he did. Behind that adoration was a hidden hysteria. Europe was at war, and America would soon be sucked in. A new kind of darkness pervaded America, subtle, often unseen, but reflected on the walls of its movie houses. The screen itself darkened and suddenly filled with shadows. It was only after the war that French film critics, deprived of American films since 1940, would notice this darkness and label it "film noir."

From Orson Welles' *Citizen Kane* to John Huston's *The Maltese Falcon* to Raoul Walsh's *High Sierra* and *They Died with Their Boots On*, there was a moodiness that hadn't been seen before in American films, a nervous twitch that hung over a scene like some portent of doom, so that we could predict Humphrey Bogart's death in *High Sierra* from the opening shots of him; disaster seemed embedded in every frame of *They Died with Their Boots On* and *Citizen Kane*. Even Walt Disney's *Dumbo* had a touch of noir, as the little band of crows sit on a wire and mock the action around them. Male stars, such as John Garfield in *The Sea Wolf* and Victor Mature in *I Wake Up Screaming*, looked like sleepwalkers upon the screen, barely able to keep their eyes open, while female stars such as Gene Tierney in

The Shanghai Gesture had a beauty so fragile it felt as if the screen would shatter around them like shards of glass.

Into this dark, ambiguous time landed the Yankee Clipper, a most unambiguous hero, like some warrior in pinstripes capable of a magnificent feat, something that could be sustained for two months and stir up a frenzy, shove that sense of foreboding away. A virtuoso of consistency during the summer of 1941, he would get at least one hit in 56 consecutive games, from May 15 until July 16, when he was robbed of two base hits by the spectacular stabs of Cleveland third baseman Ken Keltner. He then started a *second* streak of 19 games. But the numbers didn't matter so much as the Clipper's appearance day after day, his willingness to defy the demons of baseball and their stingy law of averages. Les Brown and His Band of Renown would record a hit song, "Joltin' Joe Di-Maggio," in the midst of the streak, to help Americans celebrate "Joe the One-Man Show" while the hits and home runs multiplied: he would wallop 15 homers during the streak, drive in 55 runs, bat .408.

The nation needed a one-man show that felt like it would go on forever, as if the streak itself was a kind of talisman that could keep America out of the war. As usual, no one could read DiMaggio's face. It reassured America to see that the Big Guy went about his business as calm as ever. Of course it wasn't true. "I was able to control myself. That doesn't mean I wasn't dying inside."[11]

That would always be his problem: he could show nothing except his narrowest side, and it would seem like cunning and calculation as he tried to guard his myth. When Gay Talese chased after him in 1966, all Talese could ever see was a DiMaggio without grace and charm, and he would reveal this sour man to America in "The Silent Season of a Hero."

DiMaggio wasn't so sour in 1941, but that bottling up of feeling had already given him ulcers. Still, the Bombers went on to win the pennant by 17 games, then beat Brooklyn in the World Series 4 games to 1. And on October 23, his first and only child, Joseph Paul DiMaggio, Jr., was born. He lived in a penthouse with Dorothy on West End Avenue (not far from where the Babe lived); he was more celebrated than any athlete had ever been, but it was only years afterward that his two-month stretch of hits would be immortalized as The Streak. It wasn't a powerful part of his vocabulary while he was still an active player. But as Stephen Jay Gould points out in "The Streak of Streaks," it begins to look more and more like an impossible feat.

Gould feels that a lifetime of labor means very little, "especially in sport or in battle," since "posterity needs a single transcendent event to fix [someone] in permanent memory." And DiMaggio's 56 games was such an event, "both the greatest factual achievement in the history of baseball and a principal icon of American mythology." It should never have happened, according to Gould. A streak, he says, must be absolutely exceptionless: "You are not allowed a single day of . . . bad luck." As the tension mounts, "your life becomes unbearable. Reporters dog your every step; fans are even more intrusive than usual (one stole DiMaggio's favorite bat right in the middle of his streak). You cannot make a single mistake."[12]

Still DiMaggio was able to triumph, to continue without his lucky bat until it was returned (some say with the Mafia's help). A long streak must be "a matter of extraordinary luck imposed upon great skill." It must also be a prodigious act of concentration and courage. DiMaggio had both, perhaps more than any other player; here, for once, his ability to hold in his rage kept him in good stead.[13]

It might also have been his curse, his mark of Cain. The Jolter was completely bottled up. He could never play the clown or taunt fans who had taunted him. The Babe was a performer who loved every moment of his performance. His nostrils flared at the first sign of excitement. But the Jolter was so concentrated, so deeply inside himself, that some little distraction might throw off his game. He was much more fragile than Ted Williams or the Bambino, and was wounded in some essential way. That's why the myth of DiMaggio remains with us. He was unlike any other ballplayer—he's defined by his isolation, his inability to reveal anything other than his unique and mysterious maneuvers in front of fifty thousand fans.

But the lonely outfielder who ranged in center field, who was always alone, on the field and off, could defy statistics. Perhaps some of his fierce timing came from his batting stance. Mickey Cochrane, Detroit's star catcher who played against DiMaggio in 1936 and '37, believed that the secret of DiMaggio's consistency and power was derived from "the way he keeps those wrists cocked until the final stages of his swing. . . . It's like a steel spring at work, or some form of explosion. The natural tendency is to hit too soon. [But] DiMaggio seems to wait longer than anyone I ever saw."[14]

Because of this ability to wait and watch the ball, he had fewer strikeouts than any other power hitter, whether Williams, Gehrig, Mantle, or Babe Ruth. Some baseball aficionados believe that this statistic—361 home runs vs. 369 strikeouts—is even more startling than The Streak (Williams had 521 homers and 709 strikeouts, Mantle 536 and 1,710). And DiMaggio improved on his own ratio during The Streak—15 homers vs. 7 strikeouts—which made him even more consistent and dangerous as a hitter.

Steven Jay Gould keeps coming back to the art of warfare when he describes DiMaggio's prowess in 1941, claiming that The Streak "is the finest of legitimate legends because it embodies the essence of battle that truly defines our lives. DiMaggio activated the greatest and most unattainable dream of all humanity, the hope and chimera of all sages and shamans: he cheated death, at least for a while."[15]

Gould is right, but if we rely too much on chimeras, we reduce DiMaggio's art to an act of magical powers. He may have been godlike, but he was also "the Walloping Wop," hiding his jitters as he stood there with his wrists cocked, waiting for the perfect pitch.

4.

In 1988 Michael Seidel, a professor of English literature at Columbia and lifelong baseball addict, pinpointed DiMaggio as an American icon and a mirror of what was going on in the country and much of the world as the Jolter was in the midst of his streak. "I am not charting the biography of a man but the rhythms of a legendary sequence, perhaps the most admired in sports history," Seidel writes in *Streak: Joe DiMaggio and the Summer of '41*. But in doing so, he lends a poignancy to the DiMaggio legend.[16]

"The days of the streak record the energies in a land preoccupied by war but as yet untested and unscarred by it," Seidel tells us. America was in a kind of dream state as DiMaggio rode across the public domain. He was a silent warrior in a nation on the verge of war. The gigantic footsteps and grand drama of Ruth wouldn't have worked in 1941, as "the land distrusted the self-aggrandizing bluster of the roaring twenties and the heroic figure whose demeanor suggested the flamboyance of something already done and not the steely anticipation of something yet to be encountered."[17]

The nation longed for a quieter hero. "Whether in sports, the movies, or the armed services, the image of accomplishment in the uncertain months before war drew on the intense but not the hysterical, the skillful but not the boastful, the graceful but not the mannered."[18]

And that's how DiMaggio stepped into history during the days and nights of the streak. "Baseball is played in counterpoint," Seidel tells us, as if the games themselves both quickened and quieted the nation's underlying hysteria. America searched for some consistent sign within the warlike panoply of baseball, where the outcome of a game was never really predictable. It needed a hero to tame the capricious gods and devils of the game, to accomplish the impossible in a quiet, resourceful way. And here was the Yankee Clipper, relentless in his batting stance, "head motionless and dead level," our very own dragon slayer.[19]

Had the streak happened in any other year, it might not have been so poignant or memorable, and wouldn't have reached beyond the realm of baseball. But as Seidel reminds us, "It is the cusplike quality of 1941," its dreamlike, uncertain atmosphere, "that helps account for the nostalgic strength of the year's appeal today."[20]

In the afterword to a new edition of the book, published in 2002, Seidel talks about his own "encounter" with DiMaggio on the telephone, while he was writing *Streak*. The Jolter had been reluctant to talk to any writer or researcher, who might tread upon his personal life and ask him about the late Mrs. DiMaggio, Marilyn Monroe. But Bart Giamatti, who was president of the National League at the time, had persuaded DiMaggio to talk to Seidel about the streak. DiMaggio was suspicious at first on the phone. Then he began to open up. "The legendarily silent DiMaggio was almost abuzz." And Seidel realized that the Clipper "spoke more animatedly than he had intended because he so clearly missed the era he helped to define."[21]

Seidel also realized how unkind Richard Ben Cramer had been to the Clipper in his 2000 biography. DiMaggio's misadventures were "charted without charity" in a book which made "this quiet, insecure, and somewhat sad man into a much worse human being than he was."[22]

Cramer could never quite deal with the idiot savant in DiMaggio. In reality, the Clipper had nowhere to go after 1941, not even back to baseball. The world had gotten far too ambiguous and complex for him. He wanted to live forever within the unambiguous territory defined by the streak, where he had to worry about nothing but his next hit, and where his duels with Bob Feller could hold an entire nation in its thrall. And so, in the summer of '45, before he returned to the Bronx Bombers, he brought his three-year-old son, Joe DiMaggio, Jr., to a Yankee game. People began to chant "Joe, Joe DiMaggio," until there was a tumult in the entire Stadium for "a single ballplayer whose presence embodied prewar memory and postwar relief." The Clipper was moved as he had never been moved before and would never be again. Joe Jr. smiled and said, "See, Daddy—everybody knows me."[23]

THREE

Joltin' Joe and the Ghost of Lou Gehrig

I.

Lou Gehrig lay dying while the Jolter was in the midst of his streak. There were reports that the Iron Horse was so ill "he couldn't lift a cigarette." He died on June 2, the day the Jolter had two hits against the Indians and kept the streak alive at 19 games. On June 3, in Detroit, the Tigers and the Bombers paid a silent tribute to Gehrig. "DiMaggio stood alone, facing the flag with his head bowed." He'd been fond of Gehrig, had often smoked cigarettes with him in the tunnel at Yankee Stadium—two silent men who never had the Babe's pizzazz or rollicking sense of humor. Both of them spoke in monosyllables, both brooded a lot.[1]

DiMaggio brooded all the way through the winter of '41–'42. A prince without history or antecedent, he was safe only in center field. His wife had given birth to "the year's most publicized baby"; Joe and Joe Jr. were celebrated in every newspaper and magazine. Dorothy was pictured as the model wife, Mrs. Joe DiMaggio. But there were already deep cracks in the marriage. Sometimes the great brooder wouldn't talk to her for weeks at a time. That winter, he lived at Toots' Table One rather than on West End Avenue; often he wouldn't come home at all. There was always some insult, some wound, real or imagined; if Dorothy wanted to go out to dinner in a dress with a neckline a little too low, he would rage until she wore something else, or to punish her he wouldn't go out at all. As Yankee shortstop Phil Rizzuto recalled: "Joe was rough to live with. His whole world was baseball. When you marry a beautiful woman she wants to be seen. I think Joe never really understood that."[2]

Dorothy did some brooding of her own. She ran off to Reno, and the Big Guy began to worry. As a married man with one child, he was classified 3-A—with little danger of being drafted. But if Dorothy divorced him, he would lose his deferment. He started the 1942 season in a kind of limbo and remained there. Even when Dorothy returned to West End Avenue in June, he was still in a slump. That golden warrior of '41 with his magnificent strides and batting streak was gone. And to make things worse, he had to compete with a ghost.

On July 16, *Pride of the Yankees* was released, starring his favorite actor, Gary Cooper, as Lou Gehrig. It was an enormous hit, nominated for eleven Academy Awards, and had the Babe and Bob Meusel playing themselves as erstwhile members of Murderers' Row. When Joltin' Joe had arrived like that crazy comet in 1936, Gehrig found himself "leading the league in nearly every category, including invisibility." He was no more shy than DiMaggio, yet what seemed "colorless" in him somehow made DiMaggio seem "sexy." The Iron Man had to retire in 1939, having fallen victim to a mysterious disease that was later diagnosed as amyotrophic lateral sclerosis, a debilitating illness where the muscles waste away: Gehrig got weaker and weaker until he could barely swing a bat. He died at the age of thirty-seven. The film had great appeal because it was like a war story, according to Bosley Crowther of the *New York Times*, with a hero "at the height of his glory" who is "touched by the finger of death."[3]

It mattered little to Hollywood that Gary Cooper had never played baseball, or that he was right-handed while Gehrig had been a lefty. Mogul Samuel Goldwyn simply used his own magic mirror. He let the Coop "bat right-handed and run to third base. They would have him wear a reversed Number 4 on his back. Then they would flip the film so it would look as though the actor were swinging from the left side and running to first."[4]

The Coop had just won an Academy Award playing a World War I hero in *Sergeant York* (1941), about a farm boy who becomes a terrific sharpshooter, luring Germans into the line of fire with his own turkey call. For the filmgoers of 1942, it seemed as if Samuel Goldwyn had plucked Sergeant York out of the trenches and given him Yankee pinstripes. Gehrig himself would forever wear the face of Gary Cooper. And that hulking monotonous man, Lou Gehrig, who didn't have enough verve to play Tarzan on the screen, though he auditioned for the part, suddenly had Cooper's silent power. And we watch Cooper mouth Gehrig's lines in his own Montana drawl at that mythic farewell address to a full Yankee Stadium. "Today, I consider myself the luckiest man on the face of the earth."

But DiMaggio wasn't much of a lucky man. The nation was now at war, and it longed for different heroes. Baseball would soon become a game of grandpas and stumblebums, as both stars and utility players entered the armed forces. After much brooding, the Jolter enlisted in the Army Air Corps on February 17, 1943. But he couldn't seem to function as a celebrity soldier. He was addicted to center field. Perhaps he should have become a Marine Corps pilot, like the Kid.

Ted Williams flourished during the war, broke out of his baseball mania and his protected shell, that privileged cocoon of a star.

The Kid had tried to dodge his way out of the draft, claiming he was his mother's sole support. DiMaggio had swiped '41 away from him with his hitting streak, even though the Kid had batted .406. He promised himself that he would demolish DiMaggio in '42. But there was a furor everywhere he went; polls were taken door-to-door about whether he should join up or play. "In Boston, Ted was bigger news than war in the Pacific." Finally he did enlist, though he finished out the season with the highest batting and slugging averages, the most runs scored, the most runs batted in, and the most home runs in the major leagues, while DiMaggio faltered most of the season.[5]

It wasn't only the complications of the world around him that troubled DiMaggio. He'd been a nomad, one of Toots Shor's crumb bums, and he had a hard time being a husband *and* a father. Suddenly there was another DiMaggio, Little Joe. He wasn't sure how to relate to his son. He would pose with him for some magazine and then disappear for days. And when he boasted to his pals at Toots Shor's that he could teach anyone how to hold a baby, Mrs. Joe DiMaggio muttered, "Whose baby are you going to use for teaching?"[6]

But Ted Williams didn't have a wife, and he didn't suffer at all in the service. "He loved . . . its certainty and ease." He had to deal with instructors and other apprentice pilots. His first training was at Amherst College, where he studied mathematics and navigation problems, like some freshman away at school for the first time. He became a flight instructor at Pensacola, Florida, and would have flown on combat missions had the war lasted a little longer. He didn't seem to miss baseball, or at least he never complained.[7]

DiMaggio complained from the moment he entered the army to the moment he left. His three years away from the big leagues further narrowed an already narrow man. He dined with generals, played pinochle, took part in exhibition games against army or navy teams filled with other All-Stars, other baseball refugees. It bored him to death. He would sit and brood. His ulcers got worse and he was in and out of the hospital. He was morose without his sycophants and Toots Shor. And he didn't even have Dorothy. Six months after he joined up, she filed for divorce in Los Angeles. Wrapped in a mink coat, tears in her eyes, she told a packed court that the Yankee Clipper had been cruel to her, that the arrival of Joe Jr. didn't change him at all; he still wouldn't talk to her for days at a time.

The judge was "a rabid baseball fan," and it hurt him to hear these tales of Dorothy's woes, but the Clipper still had to fork over $14,000 in cash and $150 a month in child support. He was batting zero as a husband, the papers said.[8]

He'd woo Dorothy, win her back, and lose her again, as if he were on a crazy roller coaster. He would have lost Dorothy no matter what he did, but it might have been different had he avoided that endless season of an army baseball player. Perhaps combat duty would have meant nothing to him, but without it, he amputated himself, froze his psyche. It was his last chance to leave that hermetic world of baseball, its adoration, its tight statistics, its heraldry of pennant races, and to serve with guys grounded in war. His one real tie to Babe Ruth was that neither of them had really left home. The Babe had graduated from St. Mary's to the ballpark and remained a perpetual delinquent, as if he were returning every night to his own private school for bad boys. And Joe had gone from a cloistered home in San Francisco with eight brothers and sisters to a baseball team in the Bronx that was like a cornucopia of squabbling brothers, with thousands of squabbling fans that could also have been his sisters and brothers. He spent his days wearing pinstriped pajamas like some adored, grown-up child who had this perverse gift of batting a stitched leather ball into the stands, so that every other man or boy in the country dreamt of doing the same thing. For once, he might have gotten out of that realm of baseball and lived a little with other men who had to learn how to hold a gun and battle an enemy that wanted nothing less than to annihilate you. But it never happened.

And so he suffered like an unruly child with temper tantrums. The Jolter was beside himself. He mumbled about the money he lost while away from the Yanks. But that money talk was nothing more than a mask. In a terrifying way, this hiatus from baseball was a dire prediction of what it would be like when he no longer had his haven in center field. For the first time the Jolter was utterly lost. His sense of certainty was gone, that freedom he had on the field, that controlled wildness of the Yankee Clipper. There was an aura of unreality about him; he was someone estranged from himself. Perhaps now we understood what Toots Shor's really meant to him—it was where the Jolter could unwind from the intensity of the game and also be safe within his own celebrity, adored but left alone. If people in Shor's saloon gaped at him, so what? Toots was there to protect him and that image of himself as the nonpareil. He could brood among his own peers, sit with Sinatra. Toots Shor's had become a necessary oasis.

His three years without the Yankees were also a harbinger of things to come—the squabbles with Dorothy, the jealous rages, the battle royals, and his endless need to woo her again and again served as a warm-up for his marriage to Marilyn Monroe. It was as if his armor had been torn away and he was left with nothing to fill the void of a world without baseball. He grew petulant, was full of bile, without ever being aware of what was bedeviling him. The Jolter had bedeviled himself.

FOUR

"C'mon, Joe, Talk to Me"

I.

He returned to baseball in 1946 as if he had never been away. He hit the ball like a wizard during spring training. He was much more affable, willing to smile and tell stories. But it was a masquerade; perhaps he was frightened for the first time, unsure of his skills, of his place in a postwar world. It was as if his soul had begun to rot and he'd never get out of the burden of being Joe DiMaggio. The army years had ruined him in a way, kept him even more of a child. Williams could remain a "pure" hitter, wed himself to a world of statistics, but DiMaggio was far more fragile.

Then the season started, and it was '42 all over again. He fell into a slump. He tried to woo Dorothy again, and failed. She moved into the Waldorf with a stockbroker and married him in the summer of '46, while DiMaggio sat in his room at the Edison Hotel, sat alone. Toots couldn't even coax him back to Table One. He hurt his ankle and lived with a pain in his heel. He'd never had so poor a season, batted under .300 for the first time. The Yankees sat in third place.

Their management started to panic. They had a veteran of thirty-one on their hands. They tried to palm him off on the Washington Senators, to trade him for first baseman Mickey Vernon, who had won the batting title that year. But the Senators said no. They didn't want DiMaggio. For the Yankees *and* the Senators he was now an old man.

He hobbled around in 1947, but still managed to win his third MVP. Yet '47 didn't belong to DiMaggio or Williams or any other star. It was the most significant season baseball has ever had, *almost* negating every other season from the very beginning of baseball, sometime prior to the Civil War and the formation of the National League in 1876. In 1947 the Brooklyn Dodgers took a chance on Jackie Robinson, a twenty-eight-year-old rookie with a trick knee, brought him up from the Montreal Royals, where he had been groomed, broke the "color barrier," and let him become what we all liked to think was the first black American to play in the big leagues. Thus Robinson was added to baseball's own little grab bag of myths.

He wasn't the first black player, of course. There were black Americans in professional baseball in the nineteenth century, though they were often advertised as Spaniards or Arabs; one such, Frank Grant, aka "The Spaniard," played in the high minor leagues some sixty years before Jackie Robinson ever put on a Dodger uniform. Grant, a second baseman, had to wear wooden shin guards to protect himself from runners who came at him with high-flying spikes. And two brothers from Ohio, Fleetwood and Welday Walker, played a season in the American Association, then a major league. But finally Grant and the Walker brothers couldn't play at all when bigots like future Hall of Famer Cap Anson declared that they wouldn't take the field against any team that employed a "nigger." Soon all the Spaniards and Arabs disappeared from the majors and the minors. "They are the players who just vanished from baseball's narrative, like a secret no one talks about," according to baseball historian Jim Overmyer.[1]

Black Americans had to organize their own teams, which were often phantom counterparts to the majors themselves, with the Colored Giants or the Black Yankees, and black National and American leagues. When the majors instituted an All-Star Game in 1933, blacks followed suit with an All-Star Game of their own, with big-city black newspapers in charge of the voting. Baseball Commissioner Kenesaw Mountain Landis, who had been put in place after the Black Sox scandal of 1919 to go after gamblers and clean up the game, sang to the press that the only reason black Americans were not in baseball was that they were not good enough to play against whites. And every major league owner went along with this line, even as their best and biggest stars often barnstormed with blacks during the winter, and such black players often ate them up alive.

Landis' big lie tarnished the game, left it with a terrible stink and the growing suspicion that there was a shadow world of players who might be just as powerful and fleet as the Babe or Ted Williams and Joe DiMaggio. The Babe never said one word about the blacks he played against in winter ball. But at least Williams recognized this injustice and deep insult to black Americans and raged against it. When he was inducted into the Hall of Fame in 1966, "Williams said that he looked forward to the day when such great Negro leagues players as Satchel Paige [who did get to the majors, after he was forty years old] and Josh Gibson would be elected to the Hall of Fame because 'they weren't given the chance.'"[2] Gibson, a hard-hitting catcher often called "the black Babe Ruth," not only never played in the majors but died in 1947, a sick, shrunken man of thirty-five. Yet Josh Gibson is linked with Joe DiMaggio in a sad and disturbing way.

2.

Gibson was born in Buena Vista, Georgia, in 1911, three years before Joltin' Joe. He moved to Pittsburgh as a child with his family, and became a catcher on the Crawford Colored Giants and then the Homestead Grays, who often played at Forbes Field when the Pirates were out of town; but the Pirates didn't allow the Grays to use their locker room, and Josh and his teammates had to dress and shower at the local YMCA, far from Forbes Field. Like Ted Williams, Gibson was monomaniacal about the game. He limited himself to "nothing but baseball" and led "a single-minded stilted life," according to William Brashler. He drank a lot of whiskey and gobbled tubs of vanilla ice cream.[3]

All sorts of myths have grown up around Josh; certain baseball aficionados swear he was the greatest right-handed slugger who ever lived. But how will we ever know? He never hit home runs off Bob Feller or Carl Hubbell, never played in a World Series against Joltin' Joe. We have tales about his stupendous power, how he hit line drives that "tore the gloves off infielders," that he once smashed a home run at Yankee Stadium against the Black Bombers that landed in the bullpen in left field, more than 500 feet from home plate, that he also hit "impossible" homers into the upper decks of Chicago's Comiskey Park and Washington's Griffith Stadium. He never waded into a pitch or danced on his pigeon toes at the plate like Ruth, nor did he whip his wrists like DiMaggio. "He stood flat-footed, his heavy bat gripped down to the end and held high above his right shoulder, his feet spread fairly wide apart, and with the pitch he strode only slightly—some say four inches, some say not at all, but simply raised his foot and put it down in the same spot when the pitch came," walloping the ball with the power of his upper body alone.[4]

During the war, when DiMaggio and Williams and Greenberg and Feller were all away and the big leagues were filled with stumblebums, there had been some talk about the Washington Senators signing Josh Gibson. The Senators had seen him play. They knew he might even bring them a pennant. He'd become the most famous invisible man in baseball history. But they worried that there would be a furor among the players, who like Cap Anson might stage a sit-down strike and refuse to play. And what if white fans boycotted Griffith Stadium? But even if the Senators had gathered up the courage to sign him, it would have been too late. In 1942 Josh "began a desperate slide." Gradually he grew depressed, with an endless craving for vanilla ice cream. He got dizzy when he had to chase foul fly balls, suffered from "persistent, painful headaches," often lost the power of speech, began to have blackouts and irrational outbursts of violence. He fell into a coma on New Year's Day, 1943, recovering after several hours. The doctors told him he had a brain tumor and they wanted to operate, but Josh ran from them, fearing that the operation would leave him "like a vegetable" and that he'd never play again.[5]

After more outbursts he was locked away in a ward at St. Elizabeths in Washington, D.C., the same madhouse where Ezra Pound would be held for having made rabid anti-Semitic broadcasts for Mussolini during the war. And part of Josh's own macabre history is that he would wander out of St. Elizabeths to play weekend games for the Grays.

Not even the army wanted him now, and he was given "permanent 4-F status." Finally he was let out of the hospital and lived at a boardinghouse with other Grays while the team was in D.C. He would often sit alone in a chair by the window and talk to an imaginary player: it was Joltin' Joe DiMaggio. He would repeat over and over again, "C'mon, Joe, talk to me, why don't you talk to me? Hey, Joe DiMaggio, it's me, you know me. Why don't you answer me? Huh, Joe?"[6]

Josh's sad refrain is perhaps the severest indictment of white baseball we will ever have. He could only try and seek solace from its most *visible* player, Joltin' Joe. But white baseball wouldn't talk to Josh Gibson. And its denial of him and every other black player helped contribute to his craziness. It's through Josh's own case that we can possibly comprehend how other African Americans must have suffered in their baseball ghetto. Not that black baseball wasn't its own kind of success. "It was the third largest black business in the country, behind insurance and cosmetology."[7] Never mind the relative poverty of the barnstormers. White players weren't that rich either, except for the Babe and a few others. Never mind the daily indignity of separate locker rooms and water fountains. It was the gnawing away at one's pride, the heartbreak that one could never compete, have the deep pleasure of hitting a line drive over the Clipper's head or throwing Ted Williams out at third.

A classic note of irony about black-white baseball is derived from Babe Ruth. Because of his "swarthy skin and pushed-in nose," he was often called "Niggerlips" by opposing clubs. Aware of this constant catcall, some players in the Negro leagues took great pride in Ruth and "considered him a secret brother." But Ruth was as much of a racist as those who razzed him. When called "Niggerlips" once too often, he would charge into an opponent's dugout and scream: "I don't mind being called a prick or a cocksucker or things like that. I expect that. But lay off the personal stuff."[8]

3.

Incoherent or not, riven with devils and usually half-drunk, Josh Gibson, the black Babe Ruth, became a singles hitter in '45 and '46. He continued to barnstorm and was found in the middle of one winter tour "wandering nude in San Juan." Still, he played to the very end of his life, and died on January 20, 1947, after suffering a stroke. It was only months before the start of Jackie Robinson's strange, meteoric career.[9]

Blame it on Branch Rickey, the Dodgers' president, general manager, and part owner, "a potato-shaped man in a wrinkled suit."

Known as "the Mahatma" because of his supposed idealism and religious streak, Rickey was one of the few visionaries baseball has ever had. Born in Ohio in 1881, he was a journeyman catcher (for the New York Highlanders and the St. Louis Browns) who could neither hit nor catch, but as general manager of the St. Louis Cardinals from 1925 to 1942, he was the first baseball mogul to believe in a farm system; it was much shrewder and far less expensive for a club like the Cardinals to develop its own talent rather than raid another club and steal away players at exorbitant prices. Under Rickey's tutelage, the Cardinals grew into perennial pennant winners, finding and developing players such as Dizzy Dean, Stan Musial, and Marty Marion. When he moved to the Dodgers in 1943, Rickey followed the same fashion of farm teams and helped build the "Bums" into a National League dynasty.[10]

Rickey realized that baseball was nothing but a mirror, with its own little distortions, of American society, a society shaken by the war. Blacks had been ostracized in the army and navy, often confined to segregated units, but they had fought and died alongside white soldiers, and little by little had begun to break through the military's own labyrinth of racial barriers. Sooner or later, desegregation would have to come to baseball, in spite of the owners or the reticence and ambiguity of the players themselves. And so by the end of the war, the Mahatma had already dreamed up his Great Experiment—to crash through baseball's glass ceiling and bring a black ballplayer to the majors. If he failed, if the ballplayer he chose was rejected by the Dodgers themselves, or by the other clubs in the National League, and by the fans, he would hurt the chance of future black ballplayers. And Rickey wasn't about to lose.

Even if Josh Gibson had been younger and in his prime, the Mahatma would probably not have chosen him. Josh was too volatile a player, too unsophisticated, and might have fought an entire dugout or turned morose at all the derision heaped upon his head. Rickey needed a much more subtle target, even if the target wasn't the very best prospect in the Negro leagues. He settled upon Jackie Robinson, who was a little past his prime but hadn't lived as segregated a life as Josh. Robinson had played baseball, basketball, and football against whites, was a star halfback at UCLA, with a fierce desire to win and "steely hard eyes that would flash angry in a heartbeat," according to actor Woody Strode, Robinson's teammate on the Bruins. He also served from 1942 to 1944 as a second lieutenant in the U.S. Army, where he was charged with insubordination for refusing to move to the back of a segregated military bus. He was a kind of daredevil who could deal with taunts and racial slurs.[11]

"Luck is the residue of design," Rickey loved to repeat, and it was as if he had willed Jackie Robinson into being, had welded him together with his very persona. Of course it wasn't true. Robinson was much shrewder and tougher than most of the people around him, white or black, and believed in the wonder and magic of his own possibility in spite of all the bitterness he had to face. "I went to bed one night wearing pajamas and woke up wearing a Brooklyn Dodgers uniform." But he had been in training for that transformation all his life. He would soon become the most visible man in America after crooner Bing Crosby. But he'd already been famous at UCLA. And if a tiny cabal of his own teammates was against him, he rode right over them. When the leader of the cabal, outfielder Dixie Walker, presented manager Leo Durocher with a signed petition, Durocher scoffed and said, "Wipe your ass with it!"[12]

How could the Mahatma have known that Robinson would develop into the premier second baseman of the National League? He just wanted Robinson to last the season without too many mishaps. Robinson did much more than that. He created havoc around him, confusing the opposition with his base running and his unorthodox batting style, where he seemed to chip away at the ball while he stood on his pigeon toes; Robinson seemed everywhere at once, and if he got a hit, he was capable of stealing one, two, or three bases at a time.

There had been talk of an all-out war against Robinson, a sit-down strike, but nothing came of it. Bench jockeys ridiculed him without mercy, and he continued to hit and run. One of the first players to greet Robinson on the field, to shake his hand, was Hank Greenberg, who had just been traded to the Pirates. Greenberg had been taunted from the time he joined the Tigers in 1933. Out-fielder Jo-Jo White, his own teammate, had once stared at him in amazement, believing that all Jews were supposed to wear horns. But Greenberg was a Jewish Goliath at six feet four and a half, and there weren't many players who would dare tangle with him. Also, there wasn't any Mahatma telling him not to fight back. Robinson may have become an All-Star, and certainly the most daring base runner of his time, but he paid a terrific price. He would develop high blood pressure and diabetes, and would be dead at fifty-three. Baseball had killed Jackie Robinson, even if more slowly than it killed Josh. But he was a hero in a way that Gibson could never be. Josh would remain obscure in spite of the myths that grew around him, while Robinson was the engine for one of the defining events in America in the twentieth century, played out on a baseball diamond in 1947.

4.

The season was much more mundane in the American League, which had no visionary moguls and took much, much longer to integrate, except for the Cleveland Indians, who snatched Larry Doby from the Newark Eagles—winners of the 1946 Negro World Series—eleven weeks after Robinson put on a Dodger uniform. Doby was subjected to much the same taunts and slurs but received little of Robinson's attention in the media: the *second* black American in the majors was no longer a novelty. Bench jockeys from the

Bombers probably rode him a little less than other teams did. They didn't have to. The Indians sat in fourth place, while the Yankees were the real contenders. DiMaggio was batting over .300 again, had a couple of long streaks. Crippled or not, he was the "soul" of the team. "When I turned around and saw Joe in center field, looking tense and ready for the pitch, I knew we could win, even if we were losing by nine runs in the eighth inning," said Phil Rizzuto.[13]

It hadn't been easy for the Jolter. He had two operations on his heel before the season started. He hopped around with a cane, his heel "stitched up like a bad shoemaker had fixed it." He missed the first four days of the season, had to put on a padded slipper. Then, like some gaunt ghost, he appeared at the ballpark in Philadelphia, threw himself back into the lineup, and slapped a three-run homer to win the game. The Bombers never faltered after that, even though the Jolter had to sit out a few other series.[14]

It wasn't a fabulous season for him, not in terms of the record book. For the second year in a row he failed to knock in 100 runs. But the Yankees won the pennant by 12 games, and the Jolter received his third Most Valuable Player award (one vote ahead of Williams).

The Red Sox were up in arms; they reviled the Yankees and every sports writer in America who had voted for DiMag. *Their* Kid had a stupendous season. For the second time he had won the Triple Crown, with 32 homers, 114 runs batted in, and a batting average of .343, and for the second time he was robbed, first by Joe Gordon in '42 and now by the Jolter. But Ted Williams didn't have the same fire to win. If the Thumper went 3 for 4, he would lament over his one lost hit, stuck as he was inside the world of his own statistics. But if DiMaggio had a bad day *and* the Bombers didn't win, he would blame himself and couldn't be consoled.

"If the Yankees lost, Joe thought it was his fault," recalled Toots Shor. "He'd come by on those days and would send the doorman in to get me. . . . He would stand outside and sort of hide, hoping nobody would see him. Then the doorman would come up to me and say, 'Joe's out there.' I always knew what he wanted. I would go out and we would just walk. Up and down the street, up to Fifth Avenue to look in the windows, just walk. No talking, not a word said about the game or my family or anything."[15]

Around the clubhouse or at Tootsie's he was called "the Daig," short for Dago. That's what Yankee veterans had called him when he first came up and that's what he called himself: the Dago. He had his own fan club on the team, players who adored him and began to mimic his moves, to do everything the way the Dago did. One of these worshipers was "fireman" Joe Page, a relief pitcher with an incredible fastball that jumped all over the place. His pitching (as well as his life) was wild and erratic at the beginning of the season, and he was almost sent down to the minors several times. Only the Dago could keep him calm. Page would scour the clubhouse for DiMaggio. "Where's Daig? Did anybody see the Dago come through here?" And when the fireman had the biggest win of his career, in the seventh game of the World Series (against the Brooklyn Dodgers), he said, "I knew I had to do it for Joe."[16]

That could have been the Yankee war cry in '47, right through the climactic game with the Dodgers. It was the first Series ever televised, even if it could be seen only in the bars and hotels of several eastern cities. And DiMaggio would make the one indiscretion of his entire career in front of this audience. It was during the sixth game of the Series, and the Bums were leading 8–5 at Yankee Stadium. The Jolter came up to bat in the bottom of the sixth with two men on base. He hit a long fly toward the Dodger bullpen, 415 feet away, that looked like a sure home run. Joe was already at second base when journeyman outfielder Al Gionfriddo came out of nowhere, and "in an act of God," stumbled, stuck out his glove, and caught the ball just as it was careening over the bullpen's wire fence.

And with seventy thousand fans at the Stadium and three million watching him on the tube, Joe DiMaggio kicked at the dirt near second with such power that he "smacked the base loose from its hinges," according to Yankee pitcher Eddie Lopat. No one had ever glimpsed the Jolter's feelings inside a ballpark before—the anger and the tension at a catch that was worthy of DiMaggio himself.[17]

5.

Critics generally agree that it was one of the fiercest and most evenly matched World Series ever played. It was the first time Jackie Robinson would face Joe DiMaggio on the field. The Jolter batted .231 in the Series, with two home runs; Robinson batted .259. Neither of them dominated, but it didn't matter. They were there. And yet Josh Gibson's words to Joe DiMaggio lay like a lament over the Series itself.

"C'mon, Joe, talk to me, why don't you talk to me?"

The Yanks would be one of the last teams in baseball to bring up an African American. The feeling among their owners and management was that "a black player was not a Yankee type." It was a white-bread world, full of prejudice and the fear that black players would somehow taint the Bombers, that they would suck in droves of black fans, "who would in turn scare away the good middle-class white fans."[18]

DiMaggio was a vivid part of that white-bread world, very much a Yankee of his time, entombed in the Bronx. There was never a word from Joltin' Joe about Jackie Robinson. That blindness was far more hobbling than his heel. And this is what lends such poignancy to Josh Gibson's remark. Joe's self-absorption tarnishes our sense of him as a hero and ties him to a rough-and-tumble dynasty in the Bronx that had morphed into an elitist club of white champions. There's no way in the world that Joe or any of the Yankees could ever have talked to Josh Gibson.

And what a multitude of riches and talent the Yanks would lose. In 1949 they sent their scout Bill McCorry to have a look at a young ballplayer on the Birmingham Black Barons. McCorry wasn't impressed. "I got no use for him or any of them. I wouldn't want any of them on the club I was with. I wouldn't arrange a berth on the train for any of them."[19]

That young ballplayer was Willie Mays!

The Say Hey Kid might well have been better off across Harlem River at the Polo Grounds, where manager Leo Durocher built up his own little dynasty with the help of Willie and two other veterans of the Negro leagues, Monte Irvin and Hank Thompson. But whatever Willie's fate, we're still left with the ghost of Josh Gibson. And we no longer have to hop around the usual shibboleths over how good Gibson was, whether he could have hit against Carl Hubbell, or whether his mythic home runs could have measured up to Hank Greenberg's or the Babe's. Instead, we have to scrutinize a game so colorblind before 1947 that it condemned to oblivion some of its very best players. White baseball now seems like a narrow garden, an antique world of pretense that sang its own sunny songs and fooled itself into believing it was the best.

FIVE

The Wounded Warrior

I.

It was sort of his twilight, but not quite. He couldn't hurl rockets any more from center field to home plate. Even in his fanciful autobiography, *Lucky to Be a Yankee*, first published in 1947 (and revised in '49 and '57), he wrote that his throwing arm troubled him all through 1946. "In 1947, it got steadily worse and I found that I was good for about one throw a game and not even that all the time." It's hard to believe that the rest of the league was naïve enough never to stumble onto the truth that the Jolter had a lame arm, and wouldn't have tested that arm by having runners try to stretch a single into an extra-base hit.[1]

I suspect that he still could throw a rocket when he had to, but that it hurt him with every throw (sometimes his arm was so sore after a game that Joe Page had to help him comb his hair). From 1948 on he seemed to play in constant pain, whether it was calcium chips in the elbow of his throwing arm or bone spurs in either heel. He had become the Yankees' wounded warrior, whose presence on the field was essential to the team. The warrior had to be taped up before every game. "I feel like a mummy," he said.[2]

He'd become a chain smoker and a coffee hound, would have a cigarette and half a cup of coffee between innings. He was a notorious cheapskate and wouldn't spend a dime unless he had to; whenever he visited a nightclub, somebody else picked up the tab. But he was generous with his teammates, and the few times he had dinner with them, it was always his treat. "You eat with the Dago, the Dago pays." These were often the only words he spoke during the entire evening—he was always distant, in a dark mood.[3]

Everybody seemed to want a piece of the Dago, whether it was his autograph or some sponsorship deal. "There were so many people after him, night and day, that the ball park seemed the only place he could really rest," according to Yankee third baseman Bobby Brown. But even out there in his own alley in deep center he began to look like a haunted man, someone who was already too much of a myth to play like Joe DiMag, the Daig of flesh and blood. He was the Jolter, who always had to shake and rouse, to stir something in us that no one else could. And he did.[4]

Hank Greenberg, in a documentary film about himself, swears that Babe Ruth was the only one who could mesmerize a stadium in the middle of batting practice. But he couldn't have seen the Jolter in '47 or '48. We sat like pieces of wood and watched him through the smoky haze as he took his cuts at the plate. We weren't the only ones. His teammates watched him, and so did the other players, silent in their dugout or along the foul lines, not wanting to disturb his swing. There was nothing, no game at all, not even the suspense of baseball, until the Jolter finished swinging. And the whole damn ballpark, from the smallest kid to the oldest lady, from a loudmouth car salesman to the left fielder on the St. Louis Browns, must have had a similar belief, that we were tied to DiMaggio by some taut, invisible string, that he belonged to no one in the world but us;

and we had to be vigilant: should we shut our eyes for a second, the string might break, and DiMaggio would shatter into shards of glass.

2.

He would have his best season since '41, would play as if there had never been a war, would bat .320 and lead the league in homers, 39, and runs batted in, 155. But the Yanks were caught in a three-way race with the Red Sox and the Indians; and Cleveland won the pennant in 1948 with some help from its two African American stars, Larry Doby and Satchel Paige, who claimed to be forty-one but might have been fifty. Rather than scare its white fans away, Cleveland broke all attendance records at 2,260,627 and it won the World Series against the all-white Boston Braves, 4 games to 2, with Doby batting .318.

Babe Ruth had died during the season, after suffering from throat cancer. He'd had his own battle with fame; followed everywhere, he was still a forgotten man, "creating a stir whenever he appeared in public, but curiously neutered," according to Creamer. He had wanted desperately to become a manager in the big leagues. Not a single club would hire him. The Babe believed there was a conspiracy, that he was being blackballed. He probably was. Owners were frightened of his boisterousness, of the attention he got.[5]

He had created the modern Yankees, had built the club around his own sense of bravura, his brilliance with a baseball bat and his gift for publicity. The Bombers had little use for that bravura after he retired. Yet the same Yankee moguls would honor him the moment he died, feed off the power of his myth: the bad boy of baseball was suddenly "immortal." He would lie in state at the Stadium while more than a hundred thousand fans paid their respects to the Bambino. Then his body was delivered to St. Patrick's Cathedral, where six thousand mourners were waiting for him, with another eighty thousand outside in the rain. DiMaggio was "the only active player to take part in the services."[6]

What could DiMaggio have been thinking, he who had so little power to reflect? He was Ruth's heir, the one who profited most from the Bambino's mountainous celebrity, and from baseball's need to find another such idol, different but still godlike, who could inherit *some* of Ruth's great aura. He was "the Walloping Wop" until he went away to war, the juvenile who could hit, field, and run like no other, who obscured lumbering Lou Gehrig with his feats, had the popularity of a crooner or a film star rather than a center fielder in the lonely caverns of the Bronx. Songs and jingles would be written about Joltin' Joe. And then he was shamed into joining the Army Air Corps. His wife dumped him for a stockbroker, lived in the Waldorf, and the nearest Joe ever got to battle was a heated pinochle game. He brooded, watched his career slip away, calculated the money he was losing while he was in uniform. And when the war was over, he was jolted back to baseball. He didn't know what to expect.

Still, it must have troubled him that Ruth had vanished so completely from a game he himself had transformed, so that every home run was now considered *Ruthian* or not. The Babe had been much more clever than the Yankee Clipper, much more of a showman. Yet the Yanks had relinquished him to the scrapheap of baseball history. Would the Jolter end up on the very same heap?

While he'd been in the service, baseball had transformed itself into the national myth. Every single record of attendance was broken in 1946, almost as if wartime baseball had never existed; its roster of clowns disappeared in an instant, and Joe, the reluctant warrior, was transformed into a kind of war hero. He was now even larger than the player he had been; spring training in '46 had become a circus, with the Yankee Clipper its only star; he signed more autographs than he'd ever done in an entire season of play. Who cared if he had a lousy year in '46? It reassured his fans, proved that *their* god was human, that he had as many faults as they did. And as his injuries multiplied in '47 and '48, it only added to his allure. He was their wounded warrior.

3.

And wounded he was; he'd had another operation in November 1948, to remove the bone spurs on his right heel. The operation *seemed* to be a success. He reported for spring training on March 1. The Bombers had a new manager, Casey Stengel, a fifty-eight-year-old wanderer who'd managed the Dodgers and the Braves with no success at all and had been a journeyman outfielder on five different clubs, including the Giants, from 1912 to 1925. His shoulders were hunched over and he looked like a ragged clown. He would never get along with the Jolter, called him "Mr. De-Madge," with a measure of respect and spite.

The Clipper had played under two managers for most of his career: Joe McCarthy and Bucky Harris. McCarthy respected DiMaggio right from the start. "He was the best rookie I ever saw break in. . . . Joe had this marvelous sense of anticipation. That's because he studied the game." And the Jolter had little trouble with Bucky Harris, whom he treated like a kid brother. The Bombers belonged to him, not to Bucky. Stengel was much more stubborn; hiding his venom behind a garbled language that reporters loved to call "Stengelese," he would salaam to DiMaggio whenever he hit a home run, and realized he'd never be able to rebuild the team until DiMaggio retired. But Stengel needed the Jolter right now. He couldn't knock off the Red Sox without him.[7]

But by the second day of spring training the Jolter had a noticeable limp. He would miss the season's opener for the eighth time. He had a kind of infection in his right heel that made it pulse with heat, as if there was a furnace right under the skin. He was flown to Baltimore with his inflamed heel. Reporters dogged him right inside the hospital at Johns Hopkins; wherever he was, "wheelchair patients would roll in and gawk."[8]

He appeared at opening day in his signature camel's hair coat and then withdrew inside his suite at the Elysée Hotel, would see no one except Toots Shor. The Yanks were paying him a hundred grand—more than Ruth ever made—and he had to hop around in a hotel room like some antique. He grew more and more depressed. And then, one morning in June, the Jolter stepped out of bed, put some pressure on his damaged heel, and felt no pain. The heel wasn't hot any more. And at the end of month, he appeared in the locker room at Fenway Park without warning, didn't say a word to Stengel, and trotted out to the field in a special shoe with cleatless cleats.

DiMaggio, who had missed the first two months of '49, proceeded to demolish the Red Sox, hitting 4 homers and driving in 9 runs as the Bombers swept Boston in a 3-game series. The team was suddenly alive. "One thing about Joe that nobody really understands," said Yankee pitcher Allie Reynolds. "He gave a thousand percent every game, day in and day out, for a lot of years. That takes a great deal out of a man." And in the last two games of the season, with Boston in first place, the Jolter arrived at the Stadium with walking pneumonia, played as well as a sick man could; and somehow, that limping gazelle inspired the Yanks to steal the pennant away from the Sox.[9]

He was a sick man in the World Series too, batted an anemic .111, but the Yanks still smothered the Dodgers, 4 games to 1. The Associated Press voted DiMaggio's June "resurrection"—his return to baseball on a damaged heel—the greatest comeback of 1949. It was one more accolade for the wounded warrior.

4.

Call it 1950. The Jolter was now thirty-five, and the grandpa of baseball with his hobbled heel; he still managed to play 139 games and drive in 122 runs. He had the highest slugging average in the American League at .585. But he was miserable. He had a constant battle with Casey Stengel, who wanted to platoon the great DiMaggio, have him sit out some games. "I really think Casey hated him," said second baseman Jerry Coleman. Once, while the Jolter was limping in center field, Stengel sent outfielder Cliff Mapes to replace him, but DiMaggio sent Mapes right back to the dugout with a message to Stengel: "I'll tell Casey when I want to come out." At the end of the inning DiMaggio walked right past his manager and went into the clubhouse. "I don't think they ever talked again," said Phil Rizzuto.[10]

And then, in a game against the Senators at Griffith Stadium, Stengel plucked DiMaggio from the outfield and put him on first base. The Jolter seemed terrified. He made no errors, but he stumbled once or twice, fell on his face, his uniform soaked with sweat. Stengel just couldn't understand his fear of looking bad in front of a crowd. The Jolter never played first again.

"The Ol' Perfesser," as Casey was called, did not belittle DiMaggio's brilliance. "He made the rest of them look like plumbers," Stengel once said about his star center fielder. But he wasn't out there playing with the Jolter; nor did he ever feel that particular rush of adrenalin DiMaggio could give to a team. "There was one thing about Joe that nobody ever came close to," said Charlie Keller, who played in the outfield with DiMaggio for nine years. "That was the kind of competitor he was, how he took responsibility for winning or losing, how he got the big hits in the big spots."[11]

Vic Raschi, stalwart of the pitching staff during DiMaggio's final years with the Yanks, said that "just having him out there, as sick as he was, had to be important to all of us." And outfielder Hank Bauer remembered DiMaggio's ire, how it could fall upon a teammate who fell asleep in the field. "DiMaggio never said anything to anybody about not hustling. He'd just look at you. That was enough. Nobody wanted to risk DiMaggio's displeasure."[12]

Risk DiMaggio's displeasure.

That was so much akin to his greatness. You didn't want to disappoint the Big Guy no matter who you were—a batboy, a scrub in the infield, a star at second base. Somehow he could carry a team with his concentration alone, with his fierce will, until his own powers began to fade and he was like a husk in center field with his clawless right shoe.

5.

It didn't really happen until the summer of '51. The season began and he could no longer pull the ball into his power alley in left center. The menacing swing Mickey Cochrane had talked about—that sense of a steel fist about to explode—was gone. He could only hit "piss homers" to right. "I could piss 'em right over that wall." But even piss homers were hard to find in '51. His body had started to creak like a rusty suit of armor. It hurt him every time he bent to pick up a ground ball. He would mumble to himself whenever he walked from the tunnel to the playing field, his back stooped, a dark rage burnt into his eyes. He stopped talking to reporters, and had withdrawn into a shell that was "virtually impenetrable," said Milton Gross, who followed the Bombers for the *New York Post*.[13]

But he wasn't such an enigma, after all. Someone else had become "the big thunder that spring," a blond bumpkin from Oklahoma who could hit home runs "that never came down," whack them from either side of the plate like some ambidextrous musclebound magician: his name was Mantle. Not only had he become Stengel's darling boy, but Toots Shor had been photographed with his arm around the kid. For a while the Jolter boycotted his own table at Shor's and wouldn't even answer Tootsie's phone calls. Meanwhile, Stengel crowed about his future replacement for the

Yankee Clipper: "I have my outfielder, Mr. Mantle, who hits balls over buildings."[14]

I also crowed, but for a different reason. I didn't have Stengel's Machiavellian touch, though I was a little selfish—for DiMaggio's sake, convinced as I was that he and Mantle would make a terrific duet, that the Jolter would be less lonely with Mick around. I was wrong. There wasn't a moment of rhythm between them, but a kind of civil war, as DiMaggio banished Mantle to a far corner of right field with a blistering look. But it didn't really matter whether Mantle was there or not.

The Clipper couldn't prevent his own fall. He'd become an aging behemoth, a magnificent relic. He didn't have to pretend, like Casey Stengel, to look into a crystal ball. He'd held sway over the Bronx Bombers for fifteen years; even now rookie infielder Gil Mc-Dougald would stare at him in awe and say: "It was as if you were playing with somebody you had only read about in storybooks." But that didn't stop every reporter on the Yankee beat from measuring Mantle's home runs. The kid cooled considerably after spring training and was sent down to the minors, but he still came back to haunt the Clipper: the line of succession could have been scratched into the dirt. The Babe had worn the number 3 on his blouse; Gehrig was number 4, while the Clipper had claim to number 5; and in the spring of '51 DiMaggio could see the number 6 on Mickey Mantle's back (Mantle would later switch to 7).[15]

In a slump all season, he suddenly began pulling the ball again; in a crucial series with the Indians, Bob Feller tried to rifle a fastball past the "relic," who smashed it into left-center for a three-base hit. But Durocher's Miracle Giants, who had swiped the pennant away from the Brooklyn Dodgers, seemed to have little fear of DiMaggio during the World Series; Giant pitchers threw the ball right into his gullet, and DiMaggio hit a home run over the left field wall at the Polo Grounds in game 4. The Bombers took the

Series, 4 games to 2. But there was nothing memorable about the games except that the three greatest center fielders of the modern era were all on the same field for the first and last time: DiMaggio, Mantle, and Willie Mays.

A week after the World Series, a story broke in *Life* magazine that revealed why the Giants had been so cocky about the Clipper. They had been given the scouting report that the Dodgers had prepared on the Bombers. It was a devastating critique of DiMaggio that said the Clipper couldn't field or hit or run. "His reflexes are very slow, and he can't pull a good fastball at all."[16]

DiMaggio, the great brooder, was mortified. There was no chance that he would ever step out onto the field again. When asked by a photographer friend why he was retiring so soon, he said: "Because I don't want them to remember me struggling."[17]

6.

But he had always been struggling, even when he didn't have bone spurs and could run like a gazelle. Behind all that grace was a ferocity that would have crippled most men. The Jolter wasn't *noiseless* whenever he galloped across the grass, chasing after a fly ball. "He sounded like a giant truck horse on the loose," recalled Yankee left fielder Gene Woodling.[18]

I never heard that sound from my seat in the upper deck. None of us did. I grew up a dozen blocks from the Stadium, could watch a game from the roofs of Walton Avenue, where the rich lawyers lived on their own tiny hill, but I preferred to pay the price of a ticket, at least after the Clipper returned from the war; I wouldn't have watched those wastrels who pretended to wear a Yankee uniform in '45, those ne'er-do-wells who couldn't even buy a hit off army rejects. But '46 was a different matter. I gave up my blood to go to a game. I delivered cartons of groceries that left me with a hump on my back—I was nine years old, and already the fanatic of fanatics. I knew every player in the American League. My tongue would curl around the majestic oddity of their names: Jimmy Outlaw of the Tigers, Catfish Metkovich and Rip Russell of the Red Sox, Taffy Wright of the White Sox, Zeke Zarilla of the Browns. They were much more American in their multitude than the heroes of the Revolution whose names I had to memorize for school. What were Sam Adams and that silversmith, Paul Revere, compared to the Yankee batting order?

I could see some of that batting order—Tommy Henrich, "King Kong" Keller, or Johnny Lindell—walking from their roost at the Concourse Plaza Hotel down the hill to Yankee Stadium. If there had been no Clipper, Henrich would have been my hero. He was from Massillon, Ohio, right in the middle of America. He never seemed fanciful at the plate, never showed off, and could be relied upon to start a rally that DiMaggio would finish with a double or a home run. But without the Clipper, of course, I wouldn't have broken my back to pay for that addiction. I wouldn't have gone to the Stadium at all.

My part of the West Bronx was a big Jewish garden, and I'm sure that *our* Goliath, Hank Greenberg, born and raised in the Bronx, must have had a large chunk of the Stadium devoted to his fans whenever the Tigers came to town. But I did not see them or hear them once. Perhaps I was in some blind alley where Tiger fans did not exist. None of us bothered to heckle the Jewish giant. We did not hate him. Perhaps in Detroit or in his neighborhood near Crotona Park he was the Messiah, but the guy I saw lumbered along, the different parts of his body moving with their own erratic rhythm, like some crazy machine with a cover of skin. He was thwacking home runs at an incredible clip, while DiMag was caught in a slump. We feared for the Jolter and that brooding blackness around his eyes that looked like some shimmering mask from where we sat. We worried that he might abandon baseball altogether and never show up again from his downtown hotel. We chortled with great glee when Goliath struck out, his body turning into an improbable telescope with arms and legs, or a clothes tree that had tilted too far and could not correct itself. And to tell the truth I loved to see the Clipper strike out. It was a rare event and we might wait for weeks for it to happen; considering my budget, I was lucky to see it once in a season. His body would whip around with one fluid motion, and he'd stand with his toes twisted out, stuck there for his own little eternity, as if he could take us with him into DiMaggio land, bend time to his own will, live outside the laws of batting averages, in the crispness of pure form.

But how could we have known that he would have such a hard time after he abandoned baseball, or baseball abandoned him? He wasn't really suited to become a relic. He didn't have the temperament. He couldn't pretend to be a clown, as the Babe had done. But he would be demoted to the very same scrapheap. He, who'd been one of the greatest tacticians the game had ever had, who could control the team from center field, had been bumped out of the way by a journeyman outfielder, Casey Stengel. He would brood and brood about this. Yet what role could there have been for a hero who was isolated by his own uniqueness? The Yankee management was as nervous about him as it had been about the Babe—their sway was much too large for the hucksters and showmen who had to run a club. But the Jolter had an additional burden, that blazing sensibility of his. He was so quick to wound. And without his suzerainty in center field, the Jolter would leap from wound to wound for the rest of his life, trapped by the very skills that had once sustained him. There wasn't much place for an ex-gazelle.

PART II

The Demon Lover

SIX

The Princess of Yankee Stadium

I.

Hammerin' Hank Greenberg hardly suffered when he retired from baseball after the 1947 season. He walked right out of the batter's box and into his own kind of aristocracy. He'd already married an heiress, Caral Gimbel, whose father owned Gimbel's department store; he would soon become general manager and part owner of the Cleveland Indians and then a successful stockbroker. He'd had a bit more education than DiMaggio and the Babe (he finished high school and started college), but that was not his real advantage: he was the first Jewish baseball star, which lent him an immediate cachet, and a war hero who could mingle with the upper crust of Gentiles and Jews.

The Babe also had friends in high society, but he was a renegade and a loudmouth, and the Yankees would shun him the moment he stopped wearing pinstripes. Greenberg was never a clown, Greenberg would go to the synagogue on high holidays even when the Tigers were in the middle of a pennant race, Greenberg was a *mensch*, while the Babe was unpredictable, could eat a straw hat or collect a trophy after he won a farting contest. The Dodgers might hire him as a coach to perk up their ticket sales, but they had no interest in his expertise, and he had nothing to do at the baselines but sniff the wind. He died of cancer, with a bit of a broken heart— "famous but useless," as his biographer said.

And what about the Jolter? He wasn't generous or flamboyant, like the Babe. And he wasn't much interested in heiresses. How could he mingle with the upper crust when he was always so silent? "If he said hello to you, that was a long conversation," Hank Greenberg recalled. He liked showgirls—beautiful blondes—but preferred male company at Table One: Hemingway or Jackie Gleason, who always made him laugh. Toots Shor had his own aristocracy of novelists, sportswriters, gossip columnists, athletes, and rich lowlifes. Charlie Chaplin had once showed up at Shor's with a coterie of friends and Toots treated him like a dog, told him to entertain all the other people on line. "There was fame outside Shor's, and there was fame inside," according to David Halberstam.[1]

But the Jolter couldn't spend his entire life at Table One. He had expected a job in the Yankee front office after he retired, and the Bombers brushed him off. They banished him to a television pregame and postgame show in the bowels of Yankee Stadium, where the great brooder would have to talk. He was terrified; you could see him sweat under the lights, his eyes shrinking into some island inside his head. He couldn't even pronounce his own name without glancing at a cue card. All the old grace was gone, that quickness. He was wooden inside that booth, without life, like some puppet DiMaggio, the facsimile of a former player.

His fate wasn't that different from the Bambino's; it just had prettier wrappings. He was a high-paid shill, a greeter in a white shirt, as useless as the Babe had been. Mantle and Willie Mays would follow in their footsteps, would become greeters at casinos after they retired, shills who would be tossed into oblivion, banned from representing organized baseball because of their association with gamblers. The Jolter also associated with gamblers and hoods, but he was a little more discreet, or hidden, as he always was. Richard Ben Cramer swears that Frank Costello set up a trust fund for DiMaggio at the Bowery Savings Bank, whereby nightclubs such as El Morocco or the Copa put a few hundred dollars into the till every time the Jolter made an appearance. Mob bosses in East Harlem and the Bronx "weren't at all shocked when Joe hung up his spikes. . . . They knew he didn't need the money—never would. As they said around their own kitchen tables, Joe DiMaggio didn't walk away from a hundred grand. He was walking into more than a million in cash—all safe and sound, at the Bowery."[2]

But it wasn't about money. The money was just a smoke screen. Cramer seems to think that baseball was always a business for DiMaggio, from the very first time he swung a bat for some mom-and-pop team in San Francisco, that he was looking for big bucks. I don't agree. His greed, his stinginess, his obsession about more and more money was like a constant heartburn, a disease. He was driven by pride, and money was the means of soothing him, of covering up that need never to make a mistake, to live in his own narrow world of perfection.

Unlike Mantle and Mays, he was never footloose on the field. He was the keeper of his own legend, choreographing every move. He was the first Bomber to take batting practice before a game and the last to trot onto the field, so that every spectator would be staring at him.

But he was a worrier, with ulcers, and worriers never win. He might have played another year, might have recaptured his swing, but he let Casey Stengel and the Mick drive him out of baseball. Mantle would spook him for the rest of his life—the Mick's growing fame, the injuries he suffered that were like some devotional or Stations of the Cross for his fans, the home runs, the monkey-shines, the way he would leer at women in the box seats on his route to the dugout, the hysteria in the stands that he might hurt himself again. Fans had revered the Jolter, but they couldn't love him: he was too perfect, too remote, too much like a god. The Mick was a mortal with magic powers.

The Jolter couldn't seem to shake him. He was always introduced *last* at every event, and once, at the Stadium, right after the Mick's own retirement, Mantle was introduced after DiMaggio, and the roar from the crowd was greater and longer than it had been for Joe, and he brooded for a whole year about it. When the autograph craze began, he would burn if a ball signed by the Mick brought in more than one signed by him.

It was the childish rage of a man who might have narrowed himself to invisibility—even while his grizzled pate and Pinocchio nose were recognized everywhere—if an accident hadn't happened to him. The accident was Marilyn Monroe.

2.

Of course, it was no accident on her part. She was much more calculating than the Big Guy. He loved showgirls and starlets, particularly if they were blond and didn't talk much. He was Joltin' Joe, the most famous retiree in America, and she couldn't have cared less. But she did agree to go on a "blind date" with DiMag. It was sometime in the spring of 1952. The Jolter didn't say a word all evening. He sat in his perfect polka-dot tie, and half of Hollywood came over to pay homage to him. And he didn't even realize that he was a moth trapped in Marilyn's powerful, multicolored flame.

She required a perfect prince, the Gary Cooper of baseball, an authentic American hero to smother all the flak she was getting from the recent revelation that she had posed in the nude several years ago, and that these pics that kept popping up in calendars could wreck her career. She'd also advertised herself as an orphan, and then Marilyn's mother resurfaced, a refugee from a madhouse, and it looked as if this cruel girl had abandoned her. And so the starlet who had appeared in small but memorable roles in two of the finest films of 1950, *The Asphalt Jungle* and *All About Eve*, and hopped from soundstage to soundstage in 1951, was suddenly a slut *and* a heartless daughter.

Enter Joe DiMaggio, by Marilyn's own design. Her friend and protector, columnist Sidney Skolsky, a runt who had his own office at Schwab's mythic drugstore on Sunset Boulevard (where the biggest deals were made over an egg salad sandwich at the counter), had realized like a thunderclap that no one but DiMaggio could rescue this drowning girl. And he did. Skolsky wrote about the "big blind date" in his column and planted stories wherever he could. A romance seemed to be brewing, and there were pictures of them in all the tabloids. Soon they were seen everywhere, but it still makes me suspicious. Tales abound of DiMaggio's monumental lovemaking, that he could satisfy Marilyn the way no other man had ever done, could hit home runs in the sack, as she once told Truman Capote. But we also know that she slept with other men, including Elia Kazan, while she was sleeping with the Jolter, and that she was crazily in love with Arthur Miller, whom she had met at a party in 1951.

"It was like running into a tree," she confided to her acting coach, Natasha Lytess, about meeting Miller. "You know—like a cool drink when you've got a fever. You see my toe—this toe? Well, he sat and held my toe and we looked into each other's eyes almost all evening." Miller was the most successful playwright in America, a dour, puritanical man. "It must have been like a scent of perfume in a prison cell," Mailer would say about the owlish Miller, who fled Hollywood and returned to his wife, without even kissing Marilyn.[3]

But so what? Clutching her toe could give an erotic charge greater than any kiss. She had been kissed by a hundred men,

fondled, passed around from producer to producer on the party circuit like every other Hollywood starlet. "Well, that's the last cock
I suck," she supposedly said to her lawyer after she signed her first
big contract. And even if it's an apocryphal tale, it could be true.
And so she dreamed of marrying the Owl one day, of becoming the
second Mrs. Arthur Miller, with a real home rather than a hotel
suite or a Hollywood bungalow.[4]

But she had a romance with Joe DiMaggio nonetheless. "He
wooed her sweetly," or as sweetly as he knew how. He would come
on like a house on fire, rage if she showed the least bit of cleav-
age to any man but him. She would flee from her "Slugger," as she
called him, and he would chase after her as if he were still roaming
the caverns of center field. The Jolter wore her out. He had all the
concentration and consistency of a man in the middle of a batting
streak.[5]

But soon there was a whole continent between them. The baseball season started, and he had to return to New York for the *Joe
DiMaggio Show* under the Yankee dugout. He hated every minute
of it. He'd become a collection of cue cards. He had to sweat under
the lights and ruin his best shirt and tie. He'd call her every night,
and if she wasn't there, he would fume. But she was coming east
that summer to do location shots for Henry Hathaway's *Niagara*
(1953), the film that would finally make her a star. She plays Rose
Loomis, a femme fatale in a red dress who plots to murder her husband with the help of her most recent lover. She's a woman without
mercy, wearing lipstick that's like a red wound. We see her lying
naked under a lavender sheet or else we watch her behind bump
along beneath the red dress. Most critics prefer her as the funny,
mellow vamp, Lorelei Lee, in Howard Hawks' *Gentlemen Prefer
Blondes*, where she reveals her charm as a gold digger who never really digs too hard. But I do not. Rose Loomis may be a cartoon with
a one-dimensional fury, but we've never seen this kind of displace-

ment before, as if the schizophrenia lurking under the performance is her own. "We must live two lives whenever we think of her one life," according to Mailer, or at least look for our own second skin if we want to inhabit whatever persona she has on and off the screen.[6]

She's meek and brazen, "a doe at large in blonde and lovely human form," but with a rage as deep as DiMaggio's, deeper even, since so much of his rage comes from naïveté and narrowness. He's never quite learned how to negotiate with the world beyond his own parameters in center field. He cannot, or will not, read the complexities around him. He does not want to venture very far— New York is Tootsie's, and San Francisco is the family restaurant. There's little in between. He's frustrated when the world intrudes upon his simple rules and primitive beliefs: women are either housewives or whores. And his own mad quest is to turn Marilyn into a housewife. For the Jolter, there are *enemies* all over the place, with grudges that he holds forever, or names that he scratches out of his personal phone book.[7]

Marilyn's rage is different. She'd been manhandled, made fun of, treated like a bimbo and a sexual freak who had to get down on her knees to rapacious men with a terrific talent to exploit and humiliate her. And if we consider her for a moment as a female version of Jekyll and Hyde, where she isn't the respectable Dr. Jekyll, or the monstrous libido bottled inside him, but a shivering and shy starlet, a near-waif who had to invent herself from nothing, without much education or inner resources, but with a rage almost as large as her ability to hallucinate upon a screen, an anger against those who had tried to annihilate her, to prey upon her with their own sexual fantasies and favors—and Hollywood was the land of predator producers, directors, actors, and agents—then Rose Loomis is Marilyn's means of counterattack.

One of those predators was Elia Kazan, who felt that every starlet in Hollywood was fair game. He'd sleep with Marilyn and pass her on to a friend, had even tried to give her away to Marlon Brando on the set of *Viva Zapata!* according to one of Marilyn's biographers, Barbara Leaming. But he was no fool about Marilyn. "She had a bomb inside her," he said. "Ignite her and she exploded." Still, he was blind to her power on the screen, convinced she was no more than "a charming light comedienne," and dumped her when it was convenient. "Marilyn was what she was, a delightful companion. A delightful companion is a delightful companion, not a wife."[8]

He pokes fun at her regard for Joe DiMaggio. In bed with Kazan for the last time, Marilyn confesses that her Slugger "comes all the way down from San Francisco, and we haven't even done it yet! . . . He wants to marry me, and I really like him. He's not like these movie people. He's dignified." And Kazan gives her his little poisoned kiss-off: *We made love; congratulations and farewell.*[9]

3.

The Jolter did want to marry her. He asked her all the time, certain that she would quit Hollywood and give up making films. But he couldn't really *read* Marilyn Monroe. She was a girl who lived within the crazy dance of a mirror, whose sense of worth came from the flickering light of a screen. She risked as much of herself on the movie-house wall as the Jolter had risked in center field, but he never saw it. Still, he was drawn to her fractured beauty. She had, as Mailer suggests, "a species of vulnerability that all who love her will try to describe, a stillness in the center of her mood, an animal's calm at the heart of shyness, as if her fate is trapped like a tethered deer."[10]

She was much more elusive than Dorothy had ever been; he could capture "Dottie," but not this tethered deer. He pursued her in his own fashion: "She'd shy from the pressure of his grasp . . . and he'd come on, to woo her, care for her, convince her," according to Cramer. And when the pressure became too great and she couldn't breathe, Marilyn would run from him again. But all this hustle and bustle with the Jolter didn't hurt her career. She'd never received as much attention as she did with Joe DiMaggio. Her studio, Twentieth Century–Fox, was quick to cash in on this romance. It would scize like contraband every picture of Joe visiting Marilyn on the lot, exorcize whoever else was in the photo, and present the ex-ballplayer and his blonde as the royal couple of the decade: the crown prince of baseball and the future queen of Twentieth Century–Fox.[11]

The publicity department at Fox had a real coup; Marilyn and Joe were now American royalty and they weren't even man and wife; it seemed as if half the planet worshiped them. And when she abandoned the set of *Niagara* for a weekend in the summer of '52, flew down from Buffalo to be with her Slugger in his Yankee domain, Marilyn was overwhelmed: the Yankees *and* New York had adopted her in a single day. The Jolter's pregame show was mobbed from the moment she appeared at the Stadium. "A lot of guys used to hang around that studio just to see her," remembered Phil Rizzuto. "She was really gorgeous. She'd sit in the stands before the games and talk to some of the players." Then he'd whisk her off to Table One, the little hermitage where Toots Shor wouldn't allow intruders. "Joe's a very proud and dignified guy, and he didn't like all the men looking at her. Joe is a jealous guy. But I think there is one main point to remember about Joe and Marilyn. Joe loved her."[12]

But not even love was enough. The whole city and its tabloids took pride in the fact that its very own Clipper "had sallied forth from his Manhattan cave and clubbed to (radiantly happy) submission this golden girl of Hollywood." Radiant she was and also sick to death of baseball talk and the Jolter's friends, those "strange, loud, adoring men" at Toots' saloon. He didn't seem to have any friends far from Table One or the Yankee clubhouse. And he wouldn't take her dancing, fearful as he was that someone might peek down her dress, or rub a little too close to Marilyn. High culture held little appeal. He wouldn't escort her to the theater or a museum, and would rave like a lunatic whenever she wanted to venture out on her own. "He's very sweet and kind," she confessed to a friend. "And very much a gentleman. But sometimes he's so boring I could scream. All he knows and talks about is baseball."[13]

She'd already had a bit of a fling with fashion photographer Milton Greene, a handsome gnome of a man who dressed all in black and looked a little like Peter Lorre. He shared a secret ambition with Marilyn—to have their own production company where she would not be at the mercy of Hollywood moguls such as Darryl Zanuck, who hated Marilyn but now saw her as a valuable "asset" whom he could exploit at will, lend out to another studio and reap all the profit. If she weren't tied to Zanuck and Twentieth Century–Fox, she could select her scripts and own a piece of every film she made. But it was a fanciful dream in 1952. With Joe at her side, she might have been the princess of Yankee Stadium, but no audience could see her as a femme fatale in a red dress until *Niagara* was released in 1953. She would have to wait.

And wait she did. She would have two other films released in 1953—*Gentlemen Prefer Blondes* and *How to Marry a Millionaire*—where she played "The Girl," a dizzy blonde with a babyish voice that would soon become her signature. Next Zanuck decided to throw her into a Western, *River of No Return*, directed by Otto Preminger; she feuded with him right away. Preminger told her to speak in the kittenish voice of Lorelei Lee, and when she wouldn't, he called her a whore in front of the entire crew. She became murderous on the set, and the bighearted saloon girl she's supposed to be in the film has the perverse, icy warmth of dislocation: she's utterly absent from the screen.

Now Zanuck put her in another musical, *The Girl in Pink Tights*, a remake of an old Betty Grable vehicle about a schoolmarm who becomes a singing sensation. Grable had already been discarded by Twentieth Century–Fox, and Marilyn didn't want to dance and sing as Betty Grable's ghost. She refused the role, and Zanuck had her suspended without pay and all the privileges of a star. He was willing to ruin his biggest asset. The same publicity machine that had helped create Marilyn was now prepared to destroy her. Fox's publicists planted stories with the two potent witches of Hollywood, gossip columnists Hedda Hopper and Louella Parsons, who called Marilyn unstable and hinted that she was a whore. It would have worked had Marilyn not dropped a bombshell on Hedda and Louella and the whole apparatus at Twentieth Century–Fox.

She was her own relentless publicity machine. She'd been hiding out in San Francisco with DiMaggio while the two witches tore into *La Monroe*. No one at Fox could find her. It was on January 14, 1954, when she called Fox's chief publicist to tell him she was at San Francisco's City Hall and would be marrying the Jolter within an hour.

She had made Zanuck and most of Hollywood look very small. "From the day of their marriage, she [would] become the leading female character in that great American movie which runs in serial each day in the newspapers of the world," according to Mailer. Zanuck had no choice. Marilyn had outmaneuvered him. He lifted the suspension. How could he snub the prince of baseball and his bride and not wish them well? Suddenly Marilyn had become a bigger asset than he had ever imagined.[14]

SEVEN

Mr. Marilyn Monroe

I.

How can we explain what happened next? Marilyn captured him in the whirlwind of her persona—with all its porous, vulnerable masks—and he never quite recovered. There's one little anecdote that's repeated in *every* book about DiMaggio and Marilyn. I'll steal it from Maury Allen's *Where Have You Gone, Joe DiMaggio?* We all know some little piece of the tale. The Jolter, always a practical man, was scheduled to leave on a baseball junket that January with Lefty O'Doul, his former manager on the San Francisco Seals who had remained a friend, and he decided to take his bride along and turn the junket into an extended honeymoon. It was a colossal miscalculation, but he couldn't have known. He'd been on a previous junket to Japan, where he was treated as a baseball god and called *DiMaggio-san*, and was sent on a goodwill mission to Korea (near the end of 1950); he visited hospitals and had lunch with General Douglas MacArthur. And now he was returning to Japan, still the prince of baseball, retired or not, and the legitimate heir to Babe

Ruth, or *Bay-ba Ru-tu.* He expected much the same adulation and was willing to share some of it with his bride.

But it didn't happen quite that way. Marilyn was mobbed, and he was not. While he conducted a baseball clinic, Marilyn entertained troops in Korea, visited 113,000 soldiers and Marines on ten little sorties through murderous mountainous terrain. As Maury Allen tells it:

> She . . . was thrilled as pictures of her were flashed around the world. Joe was sullen when she returned.
>
> "Joe, Joe," she exclaimed, "you've never heard such cheering!"
>
> "Yes, I have," Joe said quietly.[1]

And we're meant to chortle at Marilyn's naïveté. After all, she never once saw him roam center field and never heard the roar of seventy thousand fans after he walloped a home run against the Red Sox. Marilyn's words are a rueful reminder of what the Jolter has lost, that adulation of the crowd, the whispered hush whenever he appeared in the batter's box. But they're also Marilyn's subtle war cry, her coming-of-age in regard to Joe. Perhaps for the first time she had found her audience.

In an early draft of her "invented" autobiography, written by Ben Hecht, we can still find a glimmer of truth as she talks about singing to seventeen thousand soldiers on a windy mountaintop in her stiletto heels and lavender sheath of a dress:

> I've always been frightened by an audience—any audience. My stomach pounds, my head gets dizzy and I'm sure my voice has left me.
>
> But standing in the snowfall facing these yelling soldiers, I felt for the first time in my life no fear of anything. I felt only happy.[2]

2.

The "honeymoon" would be a disaster for Joe, the beginning and end of his marriage, as he was jolted into recognition that his wife was a bigger star than he had ever been. His illusions were stripped from him the moment he got off the plane in Japan—or rather, couldn't get off the plane, since it was held hostage by a phalanx of Marilyn's fans. The Japanese had gone ape over *Niagara*, with its femme fatale in the red dress, and Marilyn was known throughout Japan as "The Honorable Buttocks-Swinging Madam," while DiMag himself was little more than "Mr. Marilyn Monroe."

They couldn't even escape Marilyn's fans at the Imperial Hotel until she appeared on her balcony and blew kisses at them, "like I was a dictator or something."[3]

Marilyn had the time of her life in Korea. She vamped about as Lorelei Lee, sang "Diamonds Are a Girl's Best Friend" to soldiers in the remotest of camps, and said, "I'll never forget my honeymoon—with the 45th Division."[4]

It's Norman Mailer who realized that there was a robber bridegroom sitting right on top of DiMaggio's back—and it wasn't the 45th Division. "I'm going to marry Arthur Miller," she confided to Sidney Skolsky less than two months after her wedding. She'd already had terrific fights with DiMaggio upon returning to Japan from the cold of Korea. She caught pneumonia and had to camp out at the Imperial. He would have jealous fits every time a bellboy looked at her and he barred them all from the DiMaggio suite. Joe DiMaggio, the Jolter, that cunning man who combed his hair a hundred times a day, wore a spotless white shirt, could protect his own myth from intruders but couldn't control his wife: his marriage had become a battleground, with Marilyn like a general who marshaled all her artillery, all her troops. Her will was much fiercer than his, he soon learned, even if she hid it behind her blondness.[5]

Things only got worse. He'd helped Marilyn in her fight with Zanuck, had encouraged her not to capitulate, but in Tokyo he'd been little more than an appendage who fumed and finally became a nuisance.

There are photographs of her taken by Milton Greene around this time that reveal such a startling intimacy—and sensual pleasure—that it is difficult not to think of them as lovers. Certainly Marilyn's mind wasn't on Joe DiMaggio, who could no longer help her career. Lorelei Lee had made her the biggest star on the planet, and thank God she was back at work. Zanuck had thrown her into *There's No Business Like Show Business*, a musical comedy with Marilyn as a sexpot who disappears inside the decor. It was, she said, "a stupid part in a stupid picture."[6]

But it got her out of the house. She and the Slugger had rented a cottage on North Palm Drive, in Beverly Hills, high above Hollywood. Marilyn, the illegitimate little girl whose father remained a mystery to her, now lived among the stars. But it was of little solace to her. She spent most of her time at Twentieth Century–Fox in Dressing Room M—a little palace with Queen Anne chairs—on the ground floor of the beige stucco Star Building. She inherited her new quarters from Betty Grable, who had lost her crown as queen of the lot. And Marilyn had to wonder about her own career as she looked into the dressing room's multitude of mirrors.

She kept up a good front. "Joe and I want a lot of little Di-Maggios," she told reporters, while she plotted the best way to dump him. She had little free time to flirt, but she cuckolded him as often as she could, had a fling with her handsome voice coach, Hal Schaefer. And the Jolter hired detectives and thugs to follow Schaefer and threaten him. He had nothing better to do. It was the lowest point in his life, far worse than any slump. The Yanks had won the pennant without him in '52 and '53. Mantle was now the heart of the team at the age of twenty-two. Joe sat like a monk in front of the television set, watching old Westerns and waiting for Marilyn to come home from the Star Building without once realizing that North Palm Drive was a way station to her and that he, her famous husband, was little more than a transient who happened to share her bed.[7]

"He didn't like actors kissing me, and he didn't like my costumes. He didn't like anything about my movies, and he hated all my clothes. When I told him I had to dress the way I did, that it was part of my job, he said I should quit that job. But who did he think he was marrying when he was marrying me?" Marilyn would lament in a letter to Milton Greene.[8]

He had no insights into her nature. Marilyn was too complex a creature for him, too various, too volatile, and unlike Dorothy, she couldn't be tamed. He should have run to San Francisco in that Cadillac of his, with the license plate "JOE D," but he was lost. He sat still, Marilyn so deep in his blood that it was like a malignant fever. Nothing in his limited landscape could calibrate *La Monroe*. He couldn't find a workable quotient for her. He had a desperate need to simplify. Long walks with Toots could no longer soothe him. Nothing could. He never realized that Tootsie's Table One was only a subterfuge. The male company of nightclubs and saloons couldn't protect him against the whirlwind of Marilyn Monroe.

3.

He visited her on the set, frowned at her flimsy costume, and she was so perturbed that she tripped over the wiring and nearly broke her neck. She'd begun to take all kinds of pills and would stumble around in the midst of filming a scene. Hal Schaefer had to walk her "like an overheated horse" until she woke up. Nobody could understand that she had become a sleepwalker in her own marriage.[9]

In August she ran to New York to do location shots for her next film, Billy Wilder's *The Seven Year Itch*. But she couldn't escape from the Jolter. He followed her after four days and moved into her eleventh-floor suite at the St. Regis. New York was his town, after all. At least here he could sit with his cronies at Table One, dodge autograph hounds. But Marilyn had already captured New York, stolen it away from him without even trying. The town had eyes for her and her alone. According to one of Fox's publicists: "The Russians could have invaded Manhattan, and nobody would have taken notice."[10]

And so the Jolter sat and sulked, either at Table One or the King Cole bar at the St. Regis. He told his chum Jimmy Cannon about his days and nights with Marilyn, who worked like a dog, he said, "up at five or six in the morning and doesn't get through until seven at night. We eat dinner, watch a little television, and go to bed."[11]

It sounded like the description of a morgue. He never understood that he was describing the hollows of his own life, not Marilyn's. She came alive when she was without the Jolter—and she felt particularly alive on the streets of New York, in all the hurly-burly of shooting a scene, with reporters and a big crowd mingling behind the barricades or watching her from the roofs. She stood in her high heels on a subway grating, her legs otherwise bare, and a wind machine hidden under the grate drove Marilyn's dress right up to her earrings, while a hundred photographers clicked away at her crotch. "A dark patch of pubic hair was visible through two pairs of sheer white nylon panties," wrote Barbara Leaming.[12]

Who could have dreamt that a little stunt with a wind machine would create such a stir? That picture of Marilyn outside the Trans-Lux, smiling at half the world in her high heels, soon became one of the most celebrated icons of the twentieth century and catapulted her beyond the reach of all the moguls in movieland, with an innocent, joyful carnality. But perhaps it wasn't innocent at all. Perhaps the joy she expressed was the joy of being away from Joe, and the power she had to luxuriate in her own body, under the gaze of an adoring crowd. It was like her "honeymoon" with the 45th Division, a respite from marriage. Marilyn loved to be naked, felt soothed without the restraint of clothes—the different personalities that any costume imposed upon her—and here, with her dress billowing, she was as naked as she could get in front of other people.

But she never realized that she was also performing for Joe, that he was in the crowd, watching her with his own sense of doom that could eat away her joy. Gossip columnist Walter Winchell had seen his chance to goad DiMaggio, had pulled him out of his lair at the St. Regis and propelled him right into the crowd of Marilyn watchers. Joe was bewildered. He had "the look of death" on his face, according to Billy Wilder.[13]

Filled with rage, forlorn, he stumbled into Toots' saloon and told Toots what had happened, that he'd just seen his wife do a striptease right on Lexington Avenue. Then he returned to the hotel and slapped around his wife in a "famous fight" that woke up the entire eleventh floor at the St. Regis. "Joe was very, very mad with her," recalled Gladys Whitten, Marilyn's hairdresser, "and he beat her up a little bit. There were bruises on her shoulders, but we covered them with makeup."[14]

4.

It didn't matter how contrite he was. Joe was in the doghouse and remained there. Back at Beverly Hills, he was banished from Marilyn's bed and had to sleep downstairs on the couch. She would file for divorce within three weeks. They had not even been married nine months. Twentieth Century–Fox was alerted, and "the studio cavalry rode onto the scene." Poor Joe never had a chance; he couldn't get to see Marilyn; she'd moved onto the lot, slept in the Star Building, and Joe wasn't allowed near the studio. Zanuck was careful about Joe and his status as an American prince, but he couldn't have him "slugging Fox's number one asset."[15]

The studio helped her hire Jerry Geisler, movieland's most prominent criminal lawyer, who would defend Cheryl Crane, Lana Turner's teenage daughter, after she stabbed to death Lana's long-time mobster boyfriend, Johnny Stompanato. Geisler had become a sort of house lawyer to the studio and its stars. But Joe DiMaggio wasn't Johhny Stompanato, and Geisler realized soon enough that he would have to tread lightly around the Yankee Clipper if he didn't want to damage Marilyn's reputation. Like the best Hollywood director, he staged a press conference in early October outside Marilyn's cottage, dressed her all in black, as the widow of her own marriage, and talked about the conflict of careers and "this regrettable necessity" of divorce. Every step was choreographed. The bereaved bride would stumble once; Geisler would clutch Marilyn and steer her to his car, while she dabbed her eyes with a handkerchief and said, "I'm so sorry."[16]

And who was there to choreograph the Jolter? He would follow her into restaurants and make a scene. The waiters were embarrassed for the Big Guy. How the hell could they throw him out? It got even worse. He became an actor in his own pathetic comedy that was like an imitation of the Keystone Kops. He'd hired a detective to follow Marilyn around; he was always hiring detectives, had had his first wife watched while he was in the army. But this time he had an accomplice, Frank Sinatra, his old buddy from Table One. Both of them, accompanied by a pair of sleuths, burst into a building where they thought Marilyn was hiding with Hal Schaefer. But the sleuths had gone into the wrong apartment, and Marilyn got away with Hal.

Hadn't Sinatra had his own crazy romance with Ava Gardner? He was either kissing or killing her. He and the Daig were a pair of Old World charmers, with their fiefdom over women and all the privileges of male company at Table One, where women weren't really welcome unless they looked like Ava Gardner or Marilyn

Monroe. The Boy with the Golden Tonsils could also be a bit of a psychopath, beating up men or women (often without much reason) and boasting of his mob connections. Perhaps his combination of tenderness and cruelty helped make him America's number one troubadour. But DiMag didn't have golden tonsils. He could barely sing his own name. He had an old-fashioned sense of honor that Sinatra never had, was a relic even before he retired. It's hard to believe that he couldn't have hated himself at this moment, even if he had little power of reflection. He had loved a woman, loved her to death, and all he had to show was the battered-down door of some stupid apartment. He was far from the magic garden in center field where he had roamed with such assurance. He was forty years old and breaking down. The man with a world of dignity in his swing, who looked like a maestro whether he hit a homer or struck out, suddenly seemed to have no dignity at all.

EIGHT

"Bigger Than the Statue of Liberty"

I.

He survived on will alone, morphed into a demon lover who fit himself somehow into the contours of Marilyn's life. It wasn't easy. He would stalk her when she moved to New York in 1955, wait in the alleys outside her apartment at the Waldorf, pound on her door, and suffer in silence when she announced to half the world that Arthur Miller was the only man she had ever loved. But his concentration wasn't shot. The Jolter leapt onto a new center field, a much more difficult and dangerous terrain where he risked his own sanity, with few people to cheer him in the stands—there were no stands surrounding *this* center field, and he had to bump up against his shadow, make himself available when Marilyn wanted him or needed him, and disappear (or pretend to disappear) when she didn't. He'd become friendly with a ubiquitous Washington lawyer, Edward Bennett Williams, whom he had met at Toots Shor's in 1950 or '51 and who counted among his clients Mafia don Frank Costello, *Playboy* mogul Hugh Hefner, Sinatra, and the Democratic

National Committee. The Jolter would often spend Christmas with Williams at his palatial Washington home, where Williams felt Joe's agony over Marilyn. "Joe carries a torch bigger than the statue of Liberty. It has not lessened through the years. He was crazy about her."[1]

Even with that torch, he still went to the fights with Williams, Toots, and sometimes Ernest Hemingway. The crowds wouldn't leave him alone, while Hemingway often went unrecognized until one fan noticed him and his white beard and said, "Hey, you're somebody, ain'cha?" And Hemingway answered without a blink, "Yeah, I'm his doctor."[2]

But having Papa play his court jester couldn't have lessened DiMaggio's pain. It wasn't like that time with his first wife when he wanted to win her back. His epic battles with Dorothy might bring on a batting slump or feed his ulcer, but she couldn't haunt him the way Marilyn could. Dorothy had never crawled into his blood. Marilyn had broken through his wall of invincibility, that aloofness of the Yankee Clipper. Her talent for being alone was as great as his. He was a wanderer and she was a waif. And perhaps for the first time he saw *himself* in her, saw his own brooding silence in the strange mirror of her face, as if she were the private witch of Joe DiMaggio, who could work her magic on him and had little need of his fame.

He couldn't defend himself against this blond witch—she'd arouse him and bedevil him until he had no guard against her, and suddenly he wasn't the Jolter any more, wasn't the great DiMaggio but some suitor inside a country he'd never gone into before, his very own being, the widest and most mysterious of all center fields. And he, who'd never been humbled, even with a .263 batting average during his last year in baseball, even with Stengel against him and Mantle hovering behind him, had held onto his own myth until Marilyn came along and robbed DiMag of all he had ever had when she dumped him, turned him into a national joke:

DiMaggio Loses Final Game to Hollywood Goddess;
DiMaggio Run Out of Romanoff's

It was as if baseball itself, and all the precious metaphors that had sustained him so long, had betrayed the Big Guy. The language of baseball, with its hops and twists, the one language he had ever mastered, was now being used to ridicule him. It hurt the Yankee Clipper, but he didn't withdraw. He went right inside the whirlwind with Marilyn Monroe, to be with her as best he could.

2.

She turned her back on Hollywood, ran from her own fame in '55. She arrived in Manhattan as an anonymous creature, known as Zelda Zonk, without a hint of makeup and wearing dark glasses and a scarf to hide her blond hair. She enrolled at the Actors Studio, studied with Lee Strasberg, the great angry rabbi of Method Acting, whose nose bled all the time out of his ferocious hatred (and fear) of Hollywood. Of course the Actors Studio saw through her disguise, and its acolytes were immediately jealous of all the attention Strasberg gave her. Elia Kazan, Strasberg's own rival at the Studio (who'd fallen out of favor after he ratted on his fellow actors in front of the House Un-American Activities Committee to preserve his own skin as a Hollywood director), said that Strasberg was an opportunist who saw his chance to latch onto Marilyn's fame. But it's not as simple as that. She needed the angry rabbi and the little nest he gave to her at the Studio as much as the rabbi needed her.

Still, Hollywood began to poke fun of Marilyn and her desire to become a stage actress; the moguls and their publicity machines said that she was slumming at the Actors Studio—the blonde who wanted to play Dostoyevsky's Grushenka should have been dreaming about Lorelei Lee. Even Billy Wilder, the one director who seemed to understand the seriousness of her comic art, warned her against Grushenka. "Marilyn, don't play that part. Everybody's making jokes about it. You have created a great character. Stay with the character you've created. You'll be an actress and a star like Mae West. Eighty years old, you'll be playing lead parts with the character you created."[3]

But she didn't want to be Mae West or Lorelei Lee and The Girl in *The Seven Year Itch*. She had spent her whole career cultivating that image of the dumb blonde. And now she would have her sabbatical year in Manhattan, far from the studios. "If I close my eyes, and picture L.A., all I can see is one big varicose vein," she told Truman Capote.[4]

At least for a little while, she would shed the mask of a movie star, that monster known as *Marilyn*. She would meet Capote and Carson McCullers, attend parties with Marlene Dietrich and that reclusive nun Greta Garbo, have a brief affair with Marlon Brando, start her own production company with Milton Greene, talk about theater with Tennessee Williams. She could enter into Manhattan's fabric the way she never could with Joe, who had hidden her away at Yankee Stadium or at Toots Shor's with its coterie of leering men. In this other Manhattan, said Barbara Leaming, where she danced with Capote and attended classes at the Actors Studio, Marilyn was "electric with life."[5]

And it was where she bumped into Arthur Miller, whom she had not seen since January 1951. It would be like the continuation of a long fairy tale. They had their own little romance on the sly, since the Owl was still a married man. Unlike DiMaggio, who could talk about baseball as if it were poetry but had little insight into anything else, Miller comprehended the subtle savagery of Marilyn's contradictions and wants. "She had no common sense, but what she did have was something holier, a long-reaching vision of what she herself was only fitfully aware: humans were all need, all wound."[6]

But Marilyn couldn't flaunt her married prince in public. So DiMaggio was plucked out of the wings to play Arthur Miller's beard, who could escort Marilyn to the premiere of *The Seven Year Itch* at the Loew's State Theater on her birthday, June 1, 1955. Joe was obliged to walk right under a forty-foot sign of Marilyn on the subway grate, where she showed her white panties to the world. He must have been miserable all night. He threw a surprise birthday party for her at Toots Shor's right after the premiere. But how happy could she have been among Joe's comrades at Shor's saloon, amid the stink of beer and baseball? She had a fight with Joe, stormed out of her own surprise party. A photographer friend, Sam Shaw, had to take her back to the Waldorf Towers. "He loved her beyond anybody's comprehension," Shaw believed. It was after the night of the premiere that DiMaggio could be seen lurking in the shadows outside the Waldorf.[7]

Lois Weber Smith was Marilyn's press agent at the time and recalled Marilyn's difficulties with Joe while she was still at the Waldorf. Smith happened to call Marilyn once and could hear "this pounding noise" in the background. "[Marilyn] didn't refer to the noise for a while, but she could tell by my voice that it puzzled me. Finally she said, 'Oh, that's Joe banging on the door outside.'"[8]

3.

It seemed as if Joe might be banging on that same door for the rest of his life. "I am sure Marilyn was afraid of him, physically afraid. She said Joe had a bad temper," according to Smith. But I'm not sure how much Marilyn was afraid of him by 1955. She had learned to weave around his temper tantrums and to have her own curious dance with the Jolter. He was her sometime squire and dinner companion who was capable of following her in the street. But Marilyn had something else on her mind—marriage to Arthur Miller. Miller's wife had already kicked him out of the house and he'd gone off to Reno to get a divorce. Joe had been shunted aside in America's imagination; Marilyn and her long-legged Owl, Arthur Miller, would soon become the nation's number one couple. The moguls at Fox panicked when the House Un-American Activities Committee, trying to feed off the romance, prepared to flay Miller alive over his former affiliation with the Communist Party. But Marilyn wouldn't cave in to the moguls. "Some of those bastards in Hollywood wanted me to drop Arthur. Said it would ruin my career. They're born cowards and want you to be like them."[9]

Marilyn married Arthur Miller on June 29, 1956, converted to Judaism for the ceremony, and taught herself how to make gefilte fish, while Joe grew more and more obsessed with Marilyn as he fell completely out of her life. He was drinking heavily now and became a kind of predator who ran after Marilyn impersonators after having been "so publicly, famously hurt." He would wander from town to town, take in every single Marilyn Monroe act across the country, sleep with these impersonators as often as he could.[10]

Listen to Liz Renay, a burlesque star who had won the Marilyn Monroe Look-Alike contest sponsored by Twentieth Century–Fox and had written a memoir, *My First 2,000 Men*. "There were wild bed scenes" with the Jolter, "who kept trying to get glimpses of his Marilyn by looking at me." She had at least a dozen liaisons with Joe, particularly at his Mayflower Hotel suite. And when he grew sick of Marilyn lookalikes, he would go out on drunken dates with former or current Miss Americas, and once he was "so stinko" he sat on a public staircase at a Parisian hotel with Miss America of 1951, his pants unbuckled and "his member lying exposed upon his leg."[11]

That had become the world according to DiMaggio. He was no more than a common shill at "Skinny" D'Amato's 500 Club, the mob's headquarters in Atlantic City. He would appear with some Marilyn lookalike or Miss America on his arm, while people gulped at his pointy nose and the rest of him gone gaunt, and Skinny, grateful to share a bit of DiMaggio's glamour, shoved "a grand or two" into his pocket.[12]

"Golf had become his passion," according to Maury Allen. The Big Guy was bored to death. And when the nightclub circuit began to sicken him, he found a job in 1958 as a greeter and a shill for the V. H. Monette Company, the main supplier of merchandise for post exchanges on U.S. military bases throughout the world. The company's chief assets were Joe DiMaggio and Miss Americas, who traveled from base to base. "The generals and colonels were thrilled." Joe would arrive at a base on Okinawa or somewhere in France and Germany, give a couple of pointers to whatever Little League team was around, and reminisce to a bunch of officers about his batting streak—this from a man who had hardly ever talked to his own teammates.[13]

"They loved him," said Val Monette, owner of the company. "Everybody did. We would play a little golf with the commanding officers of the base, talk a little baseball and a little business, and have a grand old time."[14]

It must have been a ticket to hell for the Big Guy, brooding all the time over Marilyn. If he went far enough away, he might not have to imagine her with the Owl. But how could he have known that Marilyn was on her own ticket to hell? Her picture-book marriage to Miller had turned into a poisonous tale. The queen of gefilte fish had gone on her honeymoon to London in the summer of '56. She and Milton Greene had hired Laurence Olivier, the greatest actor of his time, to direct her in the first "child" of Marilyn Monroe Productions, *The Prince and the Showgirl*, a stale period piece without the raucous comedy that might have rescued her. Contemptuous of Marilyn, he glided around her like an oily snake. "All you have to do is be sexy, dear Marilyn," he said. She took it as a slap in the face and set about to sabotage her very own film. She would arrive later and later to devil Sir Larry, and often didn't arrive at all.[15]

But she had even more problems in the honeymoon castle Olivier had found for her and Miller near one of the queen's own parks; three weeks into her marriage she stumbled upon her husband's notebook lying open on the dining room table—Marilyn couldn't resist, and she summarized for the Strasbergs what she had read: "It was something about how disappointed he was in me, how he thought I was some kind of angel but now he guessed he was wrong." And he was beginning to agree with Olivier that she was "a troublesome bitch."[16]

She would become pregnant in England and have the first of three miscarriages while *The Prince and the Showgirl* floundered. Olivier's production assistant, Colin Clark, provides a telling footnote when he says, "What fun it might have been to make a film with Marilyn Monroe when she felt everyone around her was a friend."[17]

4.

The marriage got worse and worse. Marilyn spent the whole year of 1957 in a rage against Miller. After humiliating him at a party, she said to one of the guests: "You think I shouldn't have talked to him like that? Then why didn't he slap me? He should have slapped me."[18]

She was wounded by Miller's calculated coldness—a slap would almost have been a sign of affection. But Marilyn was no Pussycat waiting to be punished by her Owl. She didn't need Arthur Miller. She could have stayed with the Jolter if she had really wanted to be knocked around.

She hadn't forgotten the Big Guy. She kept a photo of him in her closet, and the combination on her jewelry box was 5-5-5. "I guess everybody I've ever loved, I still love a little," she liked to say.[19]

And she kept in touch with Joe Jr., treated him like a member of her own scattered little tribe. She was on the phone with him a lot, and Joe Jr. was having some problems; a roly-poly boy at a prep school in New Jersey, he always felt in his father's shadow. "JD has tried to be charming in his miserable sort of way," he would write to his mother about Joe. But his relationship with Marilyn had given him a sudden clout. He could pick up the phone and call her. "And that was one thing that put him on the map with his dad." Joe Jr. was the only conduit to Marilyn that the Jolter had while she was Mrs. Arthur Miller. Dining with generals, wandering from base to base like some Bedouin, he couldn't have known how miserable she was.[20]

It was Billy Wilder who rescued Marilyn, like some frog prince jumping out from behind his camera with the offer of a role in his new film, *Some Like It Hot*. Wilder wanted her to play "Sugar Kane," another bimbo. She signed the contract and prepared for the film by sitting in the dark and guzzling champagne. The servants marveled at her ability to stuff herself, according to Barbara Leaming. "She devoured lamb chops, steaks, hamburger, veal cutlets, and home-fried potatoes. She was particularly fond of chocolate pudding."[21]

She wailed and moaned at the first screening of *Some Like It Hot* in February 1959. "I look like a fat pig. Those cocksuckers made me look like a funny fat pig." But she failed to grasp her own unbridled magic. She wasn't fat. She was voluptuous, like a girl right out of Rubens, with a godlike ampleness and a mystery that defied the cinematic machine. "I never knew what Marilyn was going to do, how she was going to play a scene," Billy Wilder confessed. "Monroe was *always* surprising. You never knew what would come out of her."[22]

She still had to go back to her marriage . . . and the screenplay that the Owl had scribbled for her, *The Misfits*, about three modern-day cowboys and the divorcée they're involved with, Roslyn Taber, who was meant to be a reflection of Marilyn as he envisioned her, alas: she thought she would be playing Grushenka and not The Girl, but Miller's "Grushenka" was a mousy sleepwalker who drifts in and out of her dreams. The film went into production in 1960, and that's how she was on the set—a sleepwalker. "Her eyes are gone. She can't be photographed," said cameraman Russ Metty.[23]

But the inertia came from the script, not from Marilyn, and she fought with everyone, including her screenwriter husband and her director (John Huston). She wasn't even the star of the film. Clark Gable, as one of the cowboys, Gay Langland, seized whatever little force *The Misfits* had: he was no longer the romantic rebel of *Gone with the Wind* but a wrangler who rounds up horses and sells them to be slaughtered.

He would suffer a massive heart attack a day after production ended and die eleven days later. His death would haunt Marilyn for the rest of her life, as if she had murdered the man whom she had fantasized as her own father ever since she was a child.

Her marriage was over. Miller packed his bags and left before she had the chance to throw him out. She returned to New York alone, in her usual disguise as Zelda Zonk; but it was more than a disguise now. She had become an anonymous creature living in an empty apartment (Miller had taken most of the furniture). She grew profoundly depressed, reached out for whatever little lifeline she had: she'd started calling Joe even before she broke up with Miller. She couldn't eat or sleep, but fed herself "with pills, and splits of champagne," and finally, on February 5, 1961, she ended up inside the psychiatric ward at Payne Whitney. Her mother and grandmother had been locked away in a madhouse, and Marilyn must have sniffed her own doom. After three days she was allowed to make a phone call—she called Joe. He flew in from Florida and arrived at Payne Whitney in a shot.[24]

"I want my wife," he said, as if his courtship with Marilyn had never ceased, and he was more of a husband to Marilyn than Arthur Miller had ever been; he started to shake the reception desk, his neck bulging with palpable rage. Not even Payne Whitney could defy his anger or his eloquence.

5.

He would fly her to Florida, become her prince again, even if only for a little while. He went fishing with Marilyn, brought her to the Yankee training camp in St. Petersburg, where he participated as a volunteer batting instructor now that Casey Stengel was gone—the Ol' Perfesser had been fired. "His exile was over, he was back in pinstripes." Mantle was king of the Yankees now, but a very shy king who didn't get in the Jolter's way. Still, DiMaggio wasn't at ease with the new Bombers. He remained "as elegant (and bygone) as private railroad cars."[25]

And he was much more tender with Marilyn, didn't fly into jealous fits, though Marilyn still had to weave around her Slugger, pretend that she hadn't been having long hot talks with Frank Sinatra on the phone, that her poodle puppy wasn't a gift from Frank—secretly she called it "Maf" (her shorthand for Sinatra's ties to the Mafia).

And so with Maf in the middle, they fell into a quiet, low-key romance. It was like having her personal lifeguard, she told a journalist from Denmark. When she needed gall bladder surgery that summer, Joe was there; he helped her recuperate in that barren apartment of hers with its white wall-to-wall carpet and her "oceanic mess." But she felt imprisoned by Joe's constant, cloying care, and the jealousy that was becoming harder and harder for him to suppress. When he had to start visiting military bases again for the Monette Company in August 1961, Marilyn ran off to L.A. without warning Joe. It was perhaps the biggest mistake of her life. She was thinking of Sinatra and her career. "Frankie won't let me be lonely," she said.[26]

By this time she was existing in a haze of alcohol and barbiturates. Poet and playwright Norman Rosten, who was Miller's best friend and now her friend too, had seen her at the hospital and would say that Marilyn was ill, "not only of the body and mind, but of the soul, the innermost engine of desire. That light was missing from her eyes."[27]

Now Marilyn began her own dance of doom, as many of her biographers believe; she would appear in a drunken stupor at the Golden Globes in 1962, when she stumbled onto the stage to accept her award as the World's Favorite Female Star; she would be fired from her last film, *Something's Got to Give*, after her own studio declared she was insane and would never work again (meanwhile she was juggling a simultaneous romance with JFK and his brother Bobby); she would rant at Jack Kennedy like a mad witch when he dumped her after she sang "Happy Birthday" to him at Madison Square Garden in a skintight sheath; she would visit her Hollywood psychiatrist, Dr. Ralph Greenson, seven days a week, sipping champagne in the middle of each session; she would suffer blackouts and violent changes of mood while living like a vagabond and a waif in her last home, a walled-in hacienda.

Not even the Slugger could save her, though he tried. Sometimes he'd show up at her door and she'd send him away, or else she'd invite him into her hacienda that had little more than a lamp and a bed. He hired a detective to keep track of her romps with the Kennedy boys and Sinatra, who began to beat her up; and like a quiet cavalier, he'd wait outside the walls of Sinatra's compound in Palm Springs and watch over her. Even with all his patience, he was still the Jolter, with dark, murderous blood in his heart: he would never talk to Sinatra again, and would despise the whole Kennedy clan for the rest of his life.

Right after Fox fired her, he flew from London to L.A.—he was still Val Monette's "ambassador" to American military bases—

arrived at Marilyn's hacienda, and begged her to marry him; he would whisk her away from Hollywood now that she was finished with films. "And she looked at him like he was from Mars." They had a fight. The Big Guy licked his wounds and went to New York. Not even in his worst slump had he ever been so blue. He didn't want to hide out in his hotel. He ran to Toots Shor's and matched his favorite saloonkeeper "belt for belt."[28]

"What can you do with a girl like that?" he asked Toots.

And Toots said, "Aw, whaddya do with any whore . . ."

The Big Guy bolted out the door and never talked to Toots again.[29]

Her demon lover couldn't get Marilyn on the phone, but he didn't give up. He wooed her from afar—calling her and calling her—and then from up close. She couldn't resist that boyish pleading from this man with the silver hair. And she agreed to marry her Slugger again. They picked a wedding date: August 8. She ordered a wedding gown from her designer, Jean Louis, who was famous for having dressed Marlene Dietrich and Marilyn herself in the tightest of skintight gowns. Meanwhile, Joe quit his job with Val Monette, who mourned the loss. "Joe left us on August 1, 1962. . . . He told me he had talked to Marilyn and thought she had finally agreed to leave the movies and remarry him and move with him to San Francisco."[30]

And then something happened. While the Big Guy was in San Francisco for an old-timers' game in which all three DiMaggio brothers—Dom, Vince, and Joe—were reunited on the same field for the last time, Marilyn spent a wicked afternoon camped out in her own bed, swinging violently from one mood to the next until she fell into a narcoleptic sleep from which she couldn't recover. It's unclear what really happened. Did her psychiatrist, Ralph Greenson, feed her a lethal enema by mistake? Did she kill herself over Bobby Kennedy, who may have come into town and met furtively with Marilyn? Was "the President's whore" killed by a government assassin, as Joyce Carol Oates suggests in her novel *Blonde*? And was it a humdrum Hollywood actor, Peter Lawford—JFK's personal pimp *and* brother-in-law—who first found Marilyn? Or was it Greenson himself and *his* brother-in-law, Mickey Rudin (Marilyn's lawyer), who discovered the body? They didn't quite know what to do. "We took the coward's way out," remembered Rudin. "We called Joe DiMaggio."[31]

He was the one who had to identify her body at the morgue and arrange for her funeral. He was the Yankee Clipper again, back in center field, taking care of what had to be done. He would blame "the fucking Kennedys" and Hollywood itself for having killed her. He had them all blocked out of her burial at Westwood Memorial Park—Sinatra, Peter Lawford, Dean Martin, Gene Kelly—and it was bitter for Joe that she was buried on August 8, the very day they had picked for their remarriage. But he had one little consolation: it was as if they had *always* been married, that her years with Arthur Miller were just an unfortunate fluke, a trial separation from her demon lover. He wouldn't let reporters and other Hollywood ghouls into the chapel. Rudin started to cry that the Clipper was "keeping out Marilyn's close friends."

"If it hadn't been for some of those friends," the Clipper told him, "she wouldn't be where she is."[32]

And while the casket was still open he put three roses into her hands, sobbed, and sang "I love you" three times in a staccato voice that was close to incantation. In spite of his rages, his fear of her as a movie star, he had never turned her into a toy. He loved her the way he had loped around in center field, with all the godliness of a man on fire.

6.

The whole world seemed to pity him for his "famous and famously neurotic" wife, as Paul Simon once described Marilyn Monroe. Her biographers, from Mailer to Barbara Leaming, from Donald Spoto to Joyce Carol Oates (in *Blonde*), considered Marilyn a burnt-out case who either committed suicide or was shut up because, as "the President's whore," she might have known a little too much and been delusional enough to imagine herself as the First Lady. She danced at the edge of oblivion, according to Arthur Miller: "The branching tree of her catastrophe was rooted in her having been condemned from birth." Helpless and hopeless, "she was a poet on a street corner trying to recite to a crowd pulling at her clothes." And during her last days and nights "she seemed to embrace self-destruction," said Barbara Leaming. In this scenario, Joltin' Joe became a kind of sepulcher to her suicide, the schlemiel who buried his demented wife.[33]

Then there was the kiss of death from the *New York Times*. "The life of Marilyn Monroe, the golden girl of the movies, ended as it began, in misery and tragedy," according to her obit. Her death, it seems, "capped a series of somber events that began with her birth . . . and went on and on." She had a rotten family tree, with a grandma, a grandpa, and a mom who suffered from dementia. Poor Marilyn continued her mother's curse and end up a madwoman who happened to be a movie star.[34]

But something happened: she wouldn't stay dead, and we realized soon enough that our send-off was riddled with clichés. The *New York Times*, with all its interest in accuracy, claimed that Marilyn "spoke in a high baby voice that was little more than a breathless whisper," without revealing that Marilyn had appropriated this "breathless whisper." She parodied the sexual hysteria of the 1950s, made fun of America's Puritanical streak, and did it with such energy and illumination that she had no rival.

Marilyn's resurrection began in the year of her death, when Andy Warhol made his first *Marilyn* silk screens, replicating a publicity still from *Niagara* of Rose Loomis, the blond femme fatale with black eyebrows and a murderously red mouth; but for Warhol, Marilyn isn't murderous at all. He understood her playfulness and her artifice; the silk screens are a series of masks where Marilyn is always different and the same; she's both distant and near, teasing us with her own delight, forcing us not to be serious as her image fades and reappears: we cannot capture her. She has no essence. Warhol's screens replicate the movie screen with its insistence upon surface.

Warhol shoves us from the sad face of suicide, and Marilyn with her red mouth, friendly and defiant, becomes an icon all over the world. But it wasn't until 1990 that someone went into Fox's files and discovered that Marilyn wasn't a burnt-out case at all, that Fox had rehired her at a much higher salary to finish *Something's Got to Give*. During the last three months of her life she had fought back against Fox and won.

And finally, in 2004, we have a study of Marilyn that doesn't see her as a madwoman and a waif but as a phenomenally successful actress who managed her own career and might have been shrewder than we think in her romance with Jack Kennedy. "The idea that Marilyn Monroe, who had grown up in an orphanage in the Depression and fought her way tooth and nail through Hollywood to become the most desired woman in the world, might get a charge out of knowing that she was sleeping with the president of the United States, the most powerful man in the world—that she might have been 'using' him, as knowingly as he was using her—is not part of [our] myth [of Marilyn and JFK]," according to cultural critic Sarah Churchwell in *The Many Lives of Marilyn Monroe*.[35]

Barbara Leaming called Marilyn's half-naked salute to JFK at Madison Square Garden the "cry for help" of a woman who was sinking into despair. But almost fifty years later it feels like a war cry, where for the very first time a woman could confront a philandering president with the power of her own sexuality. Adlai

Stevenson, a former leader of the Democratic Party who had been shunted aside by JFK, was a witness to Marilyn's enchantment: "I don't think I had ever seen anyone so beautiful as Marilyn Monroe that night. She was wearing skin and beads. I didn't see the beads! My encounters with her, however, were only after breaking through the strong defense established by Robert Kennedy, who was dodging around her like a moth around a flame."[36]

And as we look back, Marilyn seems much more vibrant and authentic than most of the men who bumbled around her or fell into her flame—Jack and Bobby, Frank Sinatra, Sir Laurence Olivier, Elia Kazan, Otto Preminger, Yves Montand, Arthur Miller. As Norman Rosten said of Marilyn: "It may turn out that Miller was less the artist than she." He certainly was nowhere as brave or gallant. And he was far stingier than Joe DiMaggio ever was. Miller removed himself from the "hothouse" of Marilyn's emotions, her childlike vitality, thinking to preserve his own talent. But he preserved nothing at all. He should have fallen deeper into her flame and learned from her fury.[37]

It was DiMaggio who fell the deepest and couldn't recover. He was the one man who never tried to profit from her fame or steal even a little bit of her fire. He wouldn't take the two million Simon and Schuster offered him to "write" his autobiography. The Jolter knew he'd been offered that money to talk about Marilyn. He could have made much more money than Simon and Schuster's millions by signing nudie calendars of Marilyn, but he never did. Often the invitations he received were little more than tricks. Asked to Buenos Aires to reminisce about baseball, he soon discovered that the press conference had been rigged to trap him into telling stories about Marilyn. He gave every member of the press his "Sicilian stare" and stormed out of Argentina. His only song was silence.

NINE

The Greatest Living Ballplayer

I.

1962. After he buried Marilyn, the Jolter didn't come out of his house in San Francisco for six weeks. He became a recluse, surly and unforgiving with family and friends. It was this recluse that Gay Talese wrote about in "The Silent Season of the Hero." Talese revealed for the first time the man behind the DiMaggio myth— DiMaggio's private life proved to be no life at all; the guy who had guarded his image for so long suddenly had little of an image to guard. But it shouldn't have come as a revelation. That narrow man had always been there. We just never noticed it. We were too enthralled by his absolute gifts on the field and his devotion to the game. We hadn't bothered to see that there was little else to give. Talese was the first one to glimpse behind his mask. And it might have moved us, rather than repelled most readers, if only we'd understood Joe's liabilities. He'd always been absent away from the field.

Talese is never disrespectful; he worshiped the Jolter as much as most of us did, remembered that haunted face in center field. He sought the Jolter out at his San Francisco restaurant, DiMaggio's Grotto, where the recluse appeared and disappeared like "a kind of male Garbo."[1]

"I don't want to cause trouble," [Talese] said. "I think you're a great man, and . . . "

"I'm not great," DiMaggio cut in. "I'm not great," he repeated softly. "I'm just a man trying to get along."[2]

Talese should have listened. There's a terrifying lament behind DiMaggio's plea. He didn't even have the enthusiasm of a restaurateur. Unlike Jack Dempsey, he couldn't reveal a Chiclets smile and shake everybody's hand.

DiMaggio's hidden persona was swallowed up by the brouhaha that surrounded Talese's article in *Esquire*. What he told Talese seems much less cryptic now. It was 1966, and he was still in mourning, though he lived like a retired king amid a horde of sycophants who hung on his every word. He did have a poetic language—baseball—but it had no relevance beyond the range of center field. His narrowed life had robbed him of whatever curiosity he might have had. Even when he wandered near or wide, he saw nothing. Returning from a trip to Moscow in the 60s, he said: "It's OK, but you can't get a corned beef sandwich there." The man who had the eyesight of a hawk, who could spot Bob Feller's best curve by the way the stitches spun around on the ball, could not lend us one syllable about the particular fall of sunlight on the Kremlin's spires or describe the crowds in Red Square.[3]

"Don't say I'm a recluse or a hermit. It bothers me when people say that," he told one journalist. But he *was* a recluse and a hermit. For a period of nine or ten years Marilyn had pulled him out of his self-absorption, forced him to confront her needs, beguiling him perhaps but shaking him so far out of his torpor that he had to look and feel. And then he drifted back to sleep, or hid behind some insignificant mask, unless his anger was aroused—most of all against the Kennedys, who had killed his Marilyn, he said. He knew how to hold a grudge. He was good at that. Talese tells us about the time when the Jolter returned to Yankee Stadium on September 18, 1965, after the Yankees had begged Mantle not to retire—a broken man with broken knees and a batting average of .255—seduced him with a Mickey Mantle Day, as Cardinal Spellman presided over "the canonization of a new stadium saint" and fifty thousand fans cried, "We Love the Mick." There were gifts that included a Winchester rifle and a hundred-pound Hebrew National salami that had to be rolled out in a cart. And there was DiMaggio in his somber suit, like a dark prince of a former time, leading Mickey Mantle's mother to the microphone, and all the other dignitaries standing in the infield. And suddenly Senator Robert Kennedy appeared in the Yankee dugout and shook the hand of every Yankee he could find, while DiMaggio introduced Mantle as his successor in center field, "and from every corner of the stadium, the cheering, whistling, clapping came down." The Mick, as inarticulate as ever, mumbled a few words into the microphone. Then RFK came roaring out of the dugout, posed with the Mick, and shook hands with one dignitary after the other until DiMaggio stepped back and gave him a "Sicilian stare"—his evil eye—and RFK could do nothing but move down the line and reach out for someone else's hand.[4]

2.

Did the Jolter really survive Marilyn Monroe? He lived another thirty-seven years with all the trappings of success: awards, honorary degrees, money in the bank, two seasons as a coach and vice president with the Oakland Athletics, lucrative contracts as the public persona of Mr. Coffee and the Bowery Savings Bank, his service as grand marshal of several parades, and his own last seasons as king of memorabilia baseball shows. In 1969, at a dinner in Washington, D.C., to honor baseball's centennial year, local sportswriters voted him the game's Greatest Living Player by a landslide—ahead of Williams and Mantle and Willie Mays.

It was his worst misfortune after Marilyn's death. Wherever he appeared—at a banquet or charity ball, memorabilia show or Yankee old-timers' game—he had to be introduced as the Greatest Living Player, and always be the last in line so that he would have the largest echo. Perhaps he'd always been a peacock who thrived in a center field he didn't have to share. But his peacocking far from the field robbed him of some essential humanity, killed the timid streak that had once made him so appealing. The idiot savant of baseball had become a handsome sleepwalker.

In the 1970s, a few years after he had written "Mrs. Robinson" and asked us all where Joltin' Joe had gone, Paul Simon happened to meet DiMaggio at an Italian restaurant in New York. The Jolter had been upset about the song, had considered a lawsuit, and grumbled that Simon "never paid me for using my name." And he lamented to Paul Simon: "What I don't understand is why you ask me where I've gone. I just did a Mr. Coffee commercial. I'm a spokesman for the Bowery Savings Bank and I haven't gone anywhere."[5]

He couldn't understand the abracadabra of his own invisibility—that Mr. Coffee and the Bowery Savings Bank had buried him in a kind of horrible minutia. It's hard to imagine Marilyn Monroe's Slugger wanting to live this way. Why did the greatest center fielder of his time molt into Mr. Coffee? He never understood how much it diminished him. The recluse had come out of his lair as a huckster and glorified flimflam man, and couldn't see the wreckage of his own vanishing act.

The Big Guy was unconscious half the time, going through the motions, without the least spark of fire. It's no accident that Richard Ben Cramer in his biography of the Jolter skips over the years from 1963 to 1998 with the knowledge that nothing *internal* happened to the man; the mark of these years on him was as minimal as the diary he would keep, whether he visited the White House or was waiting in an airport lounge. It would even get worse as he went from memorabilia show to memorabilia show that was a peculiar kind of hell; he was a performer in his own living death and never even knew it. He'd been mourning Marilyn all along, in spite of his little flings and fixations on former Miss Americas. He missed Marilyn beyond reason—he couldn't repair himself.

His two defining roles—as "Mrs. Marilyn Monroe" and the reembodiment of Babe Ruth—had been created by others, not by him. He hadn't really captured Marilyn. She captured him, and could discard her Slugger at will. And if there had never been a Sultan of Swat, would America have hungered for Joe with such frenzy? His panoramic Stations of the Cross in center field were utterly his own, and that's what he clung to after Marilyn was gone. The only role he had left was the Greatest Living Player. And he performed it with a vengeance, like some madcap diva in a white shirt and red, red tie.

TEN

The Biggest Fan of Them All

I.

He loved to rail at Marilyn's "enemies," real or imagined. But there were very few chances in those last thirty-seven years of his life for the Big Guy to deliver a blow for Marilyn's sake. He had no more Kennedys to revile after Jack and Bobby were killed. And he couldn't worry about other phantoms. Either he was at some godforsaken kitchenware show for Mr. Coffee or accumulating caps and T-shirts and golf clubs from his celebrity tournaments until his sister Marie told him that their house on Beach Street in San Francisco would soon cave in, or cramming other T-shirts and golf carts into one of the apartments or houses in the gated communities where he lived after he moved to southern Florida to escape the California income tax. It's appropriate that his final destination in Florida was another town called Hollywood, with its own sirens of doom. Now he had more paraphernalia—ten thousand bats and baseballs in his living room—and Morris Engelberg, Esq., the biggest fan he ever had.

He met Morris in 1983. Richard Ben Cramer considers him a small-town shyster lawyer. But Morris is much more than that. He had a brand of magic that the Big Guy could not resist. He knew how to weave a spell. It was all about money, of course. The Big Guy was worried that the Bowery Savings Bank might drop him after fifteen years, and he brought Engelberg along to renegotiate his contract. They flew to Manhattan on separate planes. Morris met with "the Bowery brass," got tough, and gave them his own laws concerning DiMaggio: "You don't embarrass him, you don't trade him, and you never cut his salary. He is a Yankee."[1]

The Bowery caved in, offered Joe the sweetest contract he ever had. Morris went to celebrate with him at the Stage Deli, on Seventh Avenue. The crowd at the Stage went wild. "Joe D., Joe D. is here." Morris shouldn't have been startled: Joe's enduring power was that he was always aloof, absent even while he was present; he created hysteria wherever he went as people tried to clutch at some portion of DiMaggio.

Joe signed a $20,000 check as Morris' commission on the deal, but Morris returned the check. It was an incredible coup. Joe was constantly suspicious that others were "making money on my back." Here was a lawyer who seemed to want nothing from Joe and would soon turn him into a money machine that overwhelmed the memorabilia business. Morris liked to boast that the Clipper could earn more money in a single day signing bats than he had earned in his entire career as a Yankee, without ever comprehending that the Jolter's reign in center field had never really been about money. It had been about the absolute will of a man on fire to beat the phantoms of fate. But forlorn as he was without Marilyn and the Yankees, his appetite was endless. "Morris, I keep telling you. It's never the need of money that people do things for; it's the want of money."[2]

Want itself had become an aberration, an illness of the mind, an enfeeblement of the spirit until there was nothing left but the mania of accumulation; he wouldn't leave a restaurant without a doggie bag, attend a golf tournament without little prizes that he never opened, never used, until his apartments were graveyards of merchandise. But it wasn't so bizarre. Didn't the Greatest Living Ballplayer deserve all the paraphernalia in the world? His greed was a phantomatic quest for recognition when he couldn't really redefine himself. The Greatest *Living* Ballplayer had to be alive. After Marilyn's death, the Jolter wasn't alive at all. His signature became a kind of lifeblood that he had to guard at all cost. It was no less than a magic wand. "DiMaggio's signature on anything from a restaurant menu to a bat could bring from $150 to $2,000, and that was wholesale," Morris loved to chant. The Jolter would be filled with fury if any dealer tried to hoodwink him, get him to sign what he didn't want to sign. He's like a maddened Lear, without his daughters but with the terrible loss of his suzerainty.[3]

"The train stops here," he'd scream and walk right out of a memorabilia show. God forbid you should cross him, friend or foe. He took you "out of the phone book" and you could never get back in. His entire existence had become a series of slights.[4]

Ask him to add anything to his signature, and it was like giving away the most precious item in the world. "I ain't signing Yankee Clipper." His bats would become symbols and tokens of his esteem, and he would sign one on the birthday of whatever few friends he still had. "Morris, this is not a piece of wood, it is a piece of my history." A little before he died, he saw the alarm on Morris' face, and assured him: "I am going to make it through. There are still gloves to do."[5]

Morris was always there. Whatever we may think of him, Morris Engelberg was the one real witness to the Jolter's years in

Florida. His book on DiMaggio (written with sportswriter Marv Schneider) is a strange mix of fact, folklore, mumbo jumbo, and schmaltz. The only picture we have of the Jolter in his terrible decline is through Morris' eyes. He adored DiMaggio and made him millions. Perhaps he adored him too much. Morris believed that the bat-signing deal he arranged for DiMaggio in 1993 "was akin to Joe's 56-game hitting streak." But it was one more ghoulish ploy that robbed DiMaggio of that relentless grace he had on the field: signing 1,941 bats was a travesty of DiMaggio's magical season, whether he earned millions or not. The man who had stood alone with his fierce concentration, defying pitchers and fielders day after day in 1941, was buried alive, a moody cash cow.[6]

2.

It might never have happened had Morris not considered himself DiMaggio's son. He himself was a posthumous child, whose father died three months before Morris was born. He was a Jewish kid from Brooklyn who "desperately wanted a dad" and found him at Yankee Stadium in 1948. He would learn to walk like DiMaggio, dress like DiMaggio, until he grew into a DiMaggio clone; at six-foot-five, Morris was even taller than the Clipper himself, but in the same dark suit, whiter-than-white shirt, and red or blue tie. When Morris finally met his idol, thirty-five years later in Boca Raton, it was much more potent than love at first sight. For DiMaggio, already shrunken with scoliosis, it must have been like looking into a mirror and seeing a most peculiar version of himself. Soon they were Mutt and Jeff, a comedy team prepared to make a killing; they never once shed their conservative business suits, whatever the occasion. No matter that Morris was DiMaggio's lawyer, confidant, financial adviser, and "son." He grew into DiMaggio's schlepper, the guy who paid for his idol's haircuts, groceries, and gasoline, and every meal they had together. At memorabilia shows, Morris sat beside him, with M&Ms and Diet Coke for the Yankee Clipper.[7]

"I lived a Yankee fan's dream," whispered Engelberg, who could march through the players' gate with "the greatest living Yankee," sit in the owner's box, and feel that the clubhouse was his very own kingdom. Suppose he did exaggerate DiMaggio's worth in the memorabilia market. Mantle was as great a king of the card shows, but he never took himself or his signature seriously. "It was like Mickey Mantle had died," the Mick would moon over his retirement. He didn't want to look like DiMaggio "in those beautiful blue suits and Countess Mara ties." He wanted to disappear, and he did, while DiMaggio went on and on with his M&Ms and signature bats and balls. But he was no less forlorn than the Mick, even with all the honors. He was dreaming of Marilyn and his own death. As myopic as Morris was, he wasn't blind to DiMaggio's lament. The Clipper might go into a trance in the middle of a memorabilia show or on a fishing trip with an old friend, "and I knew he wasn't even aware he was on a boat with me. His thoughts were with Marilyn." As usual with Morris, his exaggerations and half lies hid a greater truth: the Jolter would mourn Marilyn from the day she died and would remain in mourning for the rest of his life.[8]

Morris was with DiMaggio while he lay dying of lung cancer, and according to him, DiMaggio's last words were, "I'll finally get to see Marilyn again." Somehow I don't believe him. It's a little too close to a Dickensian tale. I suspect that DiMaggio's sufferings were much more private: all Morris can describe are the doors of hell, with memorabilia shows as the different rooms of DiMaggio's endless nightmare. The Mick's nightmare was that he had failed his father, Elvin "Mutt" Mantle, who had died of Hodgkin's disease at the age of thirty-nine; he had shamed Mutt with his shenanigans, his strikeouts, his temper on the field, and his inability to become the faultless player Mutt had dreamed of; that shame would devour him, and soon his whole life was an imagined dialogue with Mutt.[9]

DiMaggio had no such dialogue with Marilyn. He was much too secretive a man. Perhaps he did hallucinate that Marilyn was still alive: while he was in the hospital, he pinched a nurse's cheek and called her his wife. But that was the confusion of a dying man. He'd been inhabiting his own tunnel ever since Marilyn died. If Arthur Miller was the robber bridegroom of his first marriage to Marilyn, as Mailer said, then DiMaggio himself was the ghostly bridegroom of the second marriage, which never took place. What did it matter if he allowed Morris into his realm as a schlepper and a clown? He had need of a clown, and what a powerful clown was Morris, who would become the sole executor of DiMaggio's estate. Cramer sees him as malicious and mercenary in each maneuver he made for DiMaggio. I do not. Morris was "protecting" the Big Guy in his own limited, unimaginative way, and he did a lot of harm, as if by releasing DiMaggio's dross—a diary that read like bird droppings—he was somehow adding to the mystery of a great man. For Morris Engelberg, *nothing* DiMaggio did could ever have been mean or small, even the doughnuts he counted religiously and wouldn't share at his memorabilia shows. Perhaps Engelberg was more cunning than I thought. The picture he offers up to us might be nothing more than a portrait of Morris himself, the portrait of a hungry man who ends up feasting on his own psyche.

But without Morris we couldn't have entered DiMaggio's hell, couldn't have conceived the Clipper's appalling nonexistence away from Marilyn. Perhaps the Jolter was only fooling himself, and his second marriage to Marilyn would have been as disastrous as the first, but at least he would have been alive.

That long, isolated watch in center field had ennobled him

somehow, lent him a kind of purity that none of Marilyn's other "husbands" ever had. Having baseballs thrown at his head humbled him, gave him a sense of limits that rarely betrayed him while Marilyn was still alive. He didn't suffer in the same way as Mantle after he retired. Mantle had an aura of unreality. The Jolter never did. He never doubted who he was or the player he had been. The DiMaggio I saw in center field wouldn't have had to carry that swaggering title of the Greatest Living Player upon his withered back. When he visited hospitals and battle areas of Vietnam in the late 1960s with Pete Rose and other big leaguers, Rose would bark at him, "Hey, the world's greatest player, let's get going," and the Jolter had just enough humor about himself to laugh. But he might not have had the same sense of humor after he moved to Florida and fell into the arms of Engelberg.

Morris encouraged the Jolter to keep a diary and keep a diary he did, stuffed with all the fulsome details of a man without a mission, who went from place to place with little else to keep him afloat but his own madness for money or his next tuna sandwich.[10]

And a concern for his grandchildren, Kathie and Paula, who weren't of his own flesh but were the adopted children of a son he despised as listless and lazy. Joe Jr. had dropped out of Yale, gone into the Marines to prove his manliness to the Big Guy, gotten married and divorced, drifted from job to job, and now had the life of a hobo without a tooth in his head. When Joe finally tracked him down, Joe Jr. ran from him and shouted, "You don't know me. You don't know who I am. Leave me alone."[11]

Joe could have been looking at the mirror image of his own face in Joe Jr.'s lament. He didn't know himself any better than he knew his son. They were both outlaws, removed from any real human connection, but Joe was an outlaw with money.

The Yankee Clipper glommed onto his granddaughters, fussed over Kathie and Paula, said he was doing all the memorabilia shows for them. Perhaps he was as sincere as so secretive a man could be, or it was just a screen for his neglect of Joe Jr. Had Marilyn not died of an overdose, she might have provided the glue to reconcile father and son—both DiMaggios were wild, stubborn creatures, each caught in his own destructive void. Without her Joe was a lone wolf in the wasteland of wherever he happened to be.

3.

When he was still a Yankee, he would walk down Fifth Avenue with his tailor, Otto Perl. "Men reached out to shake his hand, people on the other side of the street were calling his name, cars were honking their horns, cab drivers were shouting at him. And he was walking along with his big stride, smiling and acknowledging people." And as soon as he appeared in the shop, Perl's twelve tailors and all his customers would go a little crazy with delight. Perl, who had fled the Holocaust and founded his own shop in Manhattan, asked the Clipper what it took to be a baseball player in the big leagues. And DiMaggio told Perl what he had told several others.

"You have to be hungry."[12]

Now the hunger was gone, replaced by an old man's relentless want, eating a meal while he dreamt of the next, burying himself under a mountain of golf balls in his gated community until his whole life had become one vast garden with gates. This was the monotonous song of his diary—trivia rather than silence.

Engelberg did a lot damage by auctioning off the jottings of a man already demented with grief. Political satirist Andy Borowitz savaged these jottings in a little piece entitled "The Lost Poems of Joe DiMaggio," published in the *New Yorker*. Borowitz's DiMaggio is a miserable, penny-pinching pirate who stuffs his suitcase with assorted treasure—soap and washcloths swiped from phantom hotel rooms.[13]

It's a sad epilogue, almost forty years later, to Paul Simon's poignant lines about the Jolter. Has Joltin' Joe really left and gone away? Or was it just a sad retreat, the emptied hours of a hero running as far as he could from the California income tax? Whatever damage Morris might have done, DiMaggio was much, much more than the ghoulish collector described by Borowitz.

I believe DiMaggio will survive the collateral damage of his own collapse. He remains in our mythology as Marilyn's prince, who had his own beauty and needed less of hers, who followed her into the inferno of a madhouse and escaped with his blond Eurydice in his arms; with her and her alone he recaptured at least a little of that mysterious grace he had on the field, a grace beyond any notion of grandeur, as natural *and* divine as a man in a woolen shirt racing like an antelope into the endless reach of a stadium in the Bronx . . .

While revising this book, I thought of another famous recluse, J. D. Salinger, who was as much of a penny pincher as Joe D. How simple it would have been to satirize Salinger, a health nut who supposedly drank his own urine and sat like a monk in an Orgone box. Reclusive or not, he would attend church dinners in Hartland, Vermont, and sit at the head of the table "near where the pies were placed." Like DiMaggio, he would become one of the most celebrated and sought-after recluses on the planet. Salinger's seclusion had a curious spin, according to Jennifer Finney Boylan. "By the end of his life, he may have been better known for his solitude than for his imagination."[14]

"Nothing succeeds like invisibility," she tells us. "In America, we revere artists who won't do the thing they're famous for. We revere Glenn Gould, who gave up performing; Greta Garbo, who gave up acting; and Michael Jordan, who not only gave up basketball (at which he was gifted), but then, perversely, took up baseball (at which he was not)."

And, she continues, "the more steadfastly they refuse us, the more infuriatingly desirable they become," as it was with Di-Maggio. The less available he became to his fans, the more we wondered about him and recalled what it was we missed—he was the Glenn Gould of baseball, a virtuoso unto himself. We will never see another quite like him.

Finale
An Outfielder's Sky

I.

Richard Ben Cramer is convinced that DiMaggio was a disciple of Ty Cobb, one of the meanest players who ever lived. Cobb had moved to northern California after he retired from baseball in 1928 (with a lifetime batting average of .366), and kept an eye on Joe when he was with the San Francisco Seals. It was Cobb who helped Joe craft his first letter to the Yankees, who taught him to be a penny pincher and never pay for a meal. It was Cobb who told him to soak his bats in olive oil so that they would have more spring. And like Cobb, Joe was "distant, demanding toward teammates, and toward opponents purely venomous."[1]

I'm not so sure. It was Joe's concentration that often made him seem icy and indifferent. He was always in pain, long before he hurt his knees and his heels and his throwing arm: he patrolled the outfield or stood at home plate as if in the middle of some deep crisis. The Stadium's suffering Christ, he had the gallop of someone consuming himself. He wasn't "all business in baseball," as Cramer would have us believe. Like many immigrant sons he was obsessed with money, but that obsession didn't follow him onto the field. He was a morbidly sensitive man who could not bear to make a mistake. If he seemed to come out of some dark swirl and run half a mile to catch a fly ball, it was because his life depended on it—the Clipper had to get there. One of the few times he ever took himself out of a game was when he missed a fly ball because his lousy legs could no longer get him where he had to go.[2]

DiMaggio had more in common with Mantle than he ever did with Cobb. It has long been part of the Mantle legend that DiMaggio spooked him during the year they played together, that he could never look Joe D. in the eye or utter a single word in his presence. The same legend would have us believe that the Clipper's coldness to Mantle was out of pure jealousy and spite, that he was up to mischief and looking to harm him in some mysterious way—Mantle did have one of his worst injuries during the second game of the 1951 World Series when he rushed into DiMaggio country to chase after a routine fly ball hit to short right-center by Willie Mays. "I knew there was no way DiMaggio could get it so I hauled ass." But DiMaggio was parked right under the ball. And as Mantle tried to slow down in order not to bump into DiMaggio, his right shoe got caught in a sprinkler cover buried in the grass. His right knee collapsed and he plummeted to the ground. "A bone was sticking out the side of my leg."[3]

DiMaggio told him not to move.

"I guess that was as close as Joe and I had come to a conversation," Mantle would recall. "I don't know what impressed me more, the injury or the sight of an aging DiMaggio still able to make a difficult catch look easy."[4]

He would bear a grudge against the Clipper all his life, convinced that DiMaggio's showboating—his need to look good—

was the real cause of the injury. But it was Stengel's mischief, not DiMaggio's. The Ol' Perfesser had whispered into Mantle's ear that it was time to poach in DiMaggio's terrain. "Take everything you can get over in center. The Dago's heel is hurting pretty bad." But no one had bothered to tell the Dago.[5]

He'd arrived at Yankee Stadium in 1936 as batting champion of the Pacific Coast League. He knew he could hit in the majors. The fans had never seen a kid like that. He broke into the starting lineup, batted third, just before Lou Gehrig. DiMaggio felt no rivalry with the Iron Horse. Lou had welcomed him onto the club, had shielded him the best way he could: with the power of his bat. Pitchers were frightened to death of Lou. And DiMaggio saw some of the fattest pitches he would ever see while Lou was kneeling on deck, waiting to bat behind him.

DiMaggio could never shield Mantle the same way. He didn't have Lou's generosity of spirit. And by 1951 he didn't have Lou's prowess. He couldn't even pull the ball into his power alley. And his rage against himself ricocheted onto Mantle. He wouldn't help the rookie because he couldn't even help himself. He'd been a master of baseball, who could read every nuance of the game, while Mantle was the bumpkin who could hit home runs. "I just got up there and swung for the roof ever' time and waited to see what would happen." Yet his raw power had a majesty that must have shaken the Clipper, and he had a deep core of silence that was closer to DiMaggio than he would have liked to imagine. The Mick had grown up on a dirt road outside an obscure Oklahoma mining town that wasn't even on the map. His dad was a miner who had a crazy love of baseball and was himself a teenager when Mickey was born. "The feeling between Mutt Mantle and his son was more than love," according to Merlyn Mantle, Mickey's wife. "Mick was his work of art, just as much as if his father had created him out of clay."[6]

And it was this golem baseball player that DiMaggio met. "The only thing I can do is play baseball," said the Mick. "I have to play ball. It's the only thing I know." DiMaggio had to have been spooked. He would invent his own fabled meeting with Mutt that he told to Morris Engelberg (I haven't found this "meeting" mentioned anywhere but in Engelberg's book). According to the Clipper, Casey Stengel sent him on a secret mission, asked him on his way home "to stop off in Oklahoma and tell Mantle's father to lay off the kid." DiMaggio's bonus was that the Yankees paid his entire fare to Frisco. But it's hard to believe that Stengel, who despised and distrusted DiMaggio, would have sent him on a mission to Mutt. Was the Jolter simply bragging to Morris? Or was he obsessed with Mickey Mantle and Mutt? Did he wish, in his secretive, short-circuited way, that he could share something with Mutt, or that he too had had a dad who turned him into a ballplayer?[7]

2.

Mutt's early death devoured Mantle. "I dream about him all the time," he told author Peter Golenbock. He had little solace but the game itself. "When he stopped hitting home runs," said Merlyn Mantle, "the only time he had any self-esteem was after a drink or two." I met the Mick on Opening Day at the Stadium in 1985. He'd been retired for seventeen years. I was a guest of the Parks Commissioner, the real landlord of Yankee Stadium, and was invited to a luncheon party in the owner's box. There was a great brouhaha around Yankee boss George Steinbrenner. But I was interested in Mantle, who sat slumped in a corner, away from all the commotion. He had a bald spot and graying sideburns and could have been some farm machinery salesman fresh from Oklahoma in a modest blue coat. It was his first public appearance since Commissioner Bowie Kuhn had banished him and Willie Mays from baseball for having been shills in Atlantic City casinos. But they were the two most beloved players there had ever been, and fans throughout the country were in such a furor that Peter Ueberroth, the new baseball commissioner, pardoned both bad boys as quickly as he could. And so here was the Mick, hiding from himself; he seemed to have no persona other than the savage lines on his face. He was inert even when he signed a couple of autographs.[8]

I went down into the ballpark, sat behind the Yankee dugout with all the moguls. And then the Mick emerged in his old Yankee uniform and tossed the Opening Day ball; his shoulders weren't slumped and he was as visible and strong as a tree trunk. There was bedlam in the house. For a moment, this gray guy was Mickey Mantle again, a timeless quotient, the only hero who had ever lived; the roar had resurrected him. And what connects him to DiMaggio more than any other ballplayer is that they were intensely private men, with an almost pathological shyness, who came alive on the field; they loved to perform in front of a crowd, to be watched.

DiMaggio, the stingiest of men, who guarded every gesture, gave so much of himself on the field. Every game was a quest for perfection, and that quest was so exciting because he loved to perform and hated to show it; it was the tension in him that thrilled us. He would have liked to live without us but could not: *we* were his weakness, his one flaw. Mantle knew how to laugh at himself, and the Jolter did not. It crippled him to look bad. The ballpark became his own disturbing mirror; the more he hid from us, the more he revealed. We couldn't rob him of his mystery; no one could. But he let us into that secret world where baseball was a language and a law unto itself, a kind of mathematics in motion. He was the exemplar of that language, beautiful to behold. And not all the trivia of his mad diary, his so-called "lost poems," can squander his real language, perhaps the only language he ever had, that of a man whose will could bend baseball into the highest form of art.

3.

If baseball is metaphysics and magic, it is also rooted in real time, with a history that can carry us back over 150 years, whether its first game was played in Weehawken or God knows where. But one team seems to dominate that history from the time Babe Ruth put on a Yankee uniform in 1920 and reinvented the home run. In the 44 seasons from 1921 to 1964—through the eras of Ruth, Di-Maggio, and Mantle—the Bombers won 29 pennants and 20 World Series. It's no surprise that these three players should occupy so much of baseball's psychic and physical space.

Yet all three fell into their own kind of ruin after they left the Yankees, betrayed by the very organization they had helped build. Mantle and the Babe would clown, pretend to be buffoons, after baseball deserted them. DiMaggio never clowned, but the three of them were relics the moment they retired—it's almost as if Yankee management had always been suspicious of their powers and didn't want the magic they had wielded to corrupt younger players, who had to be kept in line. Suddenly they were a detriment to the Yanks.

But they were the ones who had turned the team into an all-time success story. The Bombers had become the new American royalty, with a realm that reached beyond baseball or any sport. It wasn't so much about money. DiMaggio, Mantle, and Ruth rumbled out onto the field before the era of free agents. They weren't tycoons who could compete with club owners. Mantle didn't have a dime in his pocket while he patrolled center field. He and the Jolter weren't really rich until they stopped playing and could merchandize themselves as memorabilia; it was as if they were selling their own stake in the Bombers, their own aura as world champions with their Yankee championship rings. It was a trademark no one could beat. They had created a dynasty and kept it alive.

But Mantle's era ended long before he retired. The Yankees tumbled into fifth place in 1965, sat in the cellar in 1966 for the first time since 1912, and remained a second-division team during his last season, 1968, when he was a battered mummy at the plate, bandaged up to his navel. Pitchers took pity and let him slap an occasional home run; too hobbled to roam center field, he now patrolled nothing but first base and couldn't even do that. When a Cleveland Indian rookie decided to bunt on the Mick, his own team bawled him out. "Hey," he was told, "we don't bunt on Mick out of respect for him." Like the Yankees themselves, he had become a museum piece that still played ball. The policy of blinding themselves to great black prospects such as Hank Aaron or Ernie Banks and Willie Mays had come back to haunt the Bombers. They wouldn't seize the pennant again until 1976, with a team that had more black Americans in its starting lineup than it did whites.[9]

By this time the game itself had gone through an enormous sea change, inspired by Curt Flood, a black center fielder with the St. Louis Cardinals who, in 1969, challenged the reserve clause that had kept every baseball player in bondage to his club. Having been dumped by the Cardinals after the 1968 season and traded to the Philadelphia Phillies, Flood demanded that he be declared a free agent who could negotiate with any team he desired. Commissioner Kuhn scoffed at Flood's attempt to break the reserve clause; Flood sued the major leagues and lost. His career was broken. He played a few games for the Washington Senators in 1971. The team's manager, Ted Williams, supported Flood, encouraged him to stay, but some of his teammates did not; he decided to quit the majors. He wandered for a while, lived in Majorca, returned to baseball as a broadcaster, and died of throat cancer in 1997.

But he had taken on the big leagues as DiMaggio or Mantle never did. By 1976, five years after Flood retired, owners suddenly had to deal with a scrambling world of free agents; the best players would soon become millionaires with a coterie of lawyers, investment counselors, and all kinds of witch doctors, until the players themselves were little kings. It's no accident that the nostalgia craze began in the 1980s: DiMaggio and Mantle had become antiques, heroes out of a kinder past when baseball wasn't about being a millionaire, when half the roster consisted of stumblebums who needed a second job. Perhaps Mick and the Jolter had been just as obsessed about money, but they weren't self-contained corporations that floated onto the field with a leather glove.

Baseball is now a Bunyanesque world of startling increase and excess; it's not money alone that has multiplied, but the whole idea of *possibility*. Poor Roger Maris became a pariah when he broke the Babe's record of 60 home runs (for one season) in 1961; but nobody mourned when Mark McGwire, looking more and more like a bull or a bionic man, slapped 70 home runs for the St. Louis Cardinals in 1998. And then baseball pilloried him when the steroid scandal broke, and until recently McGwire had to live like a recluse, "the Howard Hughes of baseball." For a few seasons he was the most exciting batter in the big leagues, but he may never be elected to the Hall of Fame, even though every single player and every single fan conspired with Mark McGwire. As outfielder Tony Gwynn, elected to the Hall in 2007, said of the rampant use of steroids in the major leagues: "We all knew. All you all knew. We knew. Players knew. Owners knew. Everybody knew. And we didn't say anything about it."[10]

We all worshiped the same gods of excess, as if we dreamt of a whole country of Babe Ruths, forgetting that there had been only *one* Babe, *one* Mantle, *one* DiMaggio, not a surfeit of them like pets in a gigantic collection box. Rather, they remain powerful ghosts in some hidden arena, haunting us, joggling our minds. David Halberstam believed it was radio that added to the Jolter's allure. "It is no coincidence that DiMaggio's fame was so lasting, and that he was the last great hero of the radio era," who didn't have to suffer that curious reduction of the little tube.[11] But I'm not convinced.

He was no less a god when I watched him on TV for the first time in 1947, from the window of a neighborhood bar. He was unlike any other ballplayer; even the dull grimness of television couldn't spoil DiMaggio; he stood in center field along some invisible line, with a terrifying tightness, until he leapt into motion without the least warning, the whole of him unfurling like a relentless spring.

But this silent and secretive man didn't owe us that same authenticity off the field. We just couldn't believe that the Jolter wanted so little to do with us. He was the kind of "Isolato" whom Herman Melville often wrote about, an Ishmael with a baseball bat, who fell in love with Marilyn Monroe, came out of his dark corner for a little while, and went back in after she died. We shouldn't have to punish him for that.

He gave us what he could: the gift of his game. Once, when sitting with Henry Kissinger in the owner's box at Yankee Stadium, the ever-silent DiMaggio burst into chatter about a left-handed relief pitcher who had been brought in to replace another left-hander. Both lefties seemed the same to Kissinger. "No, look," said the Jolter. "It's a different arm angle. You gotta look at the release point. See this guy comes three quarters, he's gonna curve you on the outside—unless you move up a little, get the bat out to hit it before the break."[12]

DiMaggio's art was all about the violence of form, the breaking of some imaginary scrim, going suddenly from silence into song and back into silence again. He had a nervous poetry on the field that no one else had—a lonely lyricism that jolted us out of our seats. That's why we celebrate him seventy-five years after he first started to patrol center field—never a rookie, and never really retired.

4.

Sportswriter, novelist, and baseball fan Bob Lipsyte has his own story to tell about the Jolter, whom he met more than once. In the mid-eighties, when DiMaggio was already so misanthropic, with a lifelong reticence about most reporters, he agreed to sit for an interview with "Lippy," as he liked to call Lipsyte with a kind of rough affection. Bob cringed at the mention of that nickname. "I spilled a lot of blood as a kid not to have people call me Lippy."[13]

But he had to forgive the Jolter. It was Old Timers' Day at Yankee Stadium, and Bob showed up an hour before the old-timers' game, as scheduled. The Jolter wasn't wearing pinstripes. "He was fully dressed," in his signature white shirt, impeccable suit and tie. And he sat around, "tapping his toe."

"Where were you, Lippy? I've been waiting for you half an hour," he said, though Bob was barely a minute late.

The loudspeakers were crackling, and Bob couldn't even hear himself talk. The Jolter picked up a mobile phone and barked into it. Bob had no idea whom he called, but the loudspeakers went dead and stayed dead during the entire interview. Yet, as Bob remembers, the static hadn't come from the loudspeakers alone. "DiMaggio had nothing to say."

He'd grown into a man of one too many masks. But Bob had also met him sometime in the sixties, when the Jolter served as "an honorary hitting instructor" at the Yankees' Florida training camp. He was still mourning Marilyn Monroe, and no one dared approach him. "He was there to be looked at. You were not supposed to talk to him."

But one cold day that spring, when the ground was so wet that planks were put across the infield, Bob and the Jolter "almost bumped heads . . . both our heads jerked up. He had a startled look in his eye. He was sure I was going to say something about Marilyn."

Bob looked at the sky and said to the Jolter: "I guess this is not a good day to play the outfield."

"It's not true," DiMaggio told him. "That's an outfielder's sky."

And the Jolter began to rattle off a litany of problems and conditions that an outfielder had to face: *Wind, sun, lights . . .* "It was like talking to Michelangelo about the decisions he made for the Sistine Chapel," Bob recalled.

Seeing Bob shiver in the cold, DiMaggio shouted at one of the younger Yankee players. "Rook, give my friend Lippy your jacket."

That was about as intimate as the Jolter could get. Bob was a Yankee fan, but he didn't see his first game until he was thirteen. And when I asked him whether DiMaggio has remained an icon for him, he said: "An icon, yeah, like someone in a photograph that's fading. . . . He was so tightly buttoned."

Bob talked about "the beauty of his movements. He'll always be a kind of Baryshnikov—not Nureyev. His timing was impeccable. Mantle was much more of a human story. He was flawed in ways we can relate to and understand; his flaws hobbled him. DiMaggio's flaws made him a better player.

"Mantle has an enormous emotional pull. With DiMaggio, it was as if someone wheeled in a statue of [Michelangelo's] David; everyone gasped at his beauty. But you didn't cry."

Yet the Jolter's charisma lay in the distance he demanded between him and us. He was there to be looked at and to knock our breath away. Mantle never had that power over us.

"Our emotion about Mantle," our connection to him, "was based on not knowing him. The man was a stone prick. But there were interesting grooves and depths in DiMaggio. DiMaggio was capable of surprising."

If he couldn't make us cry, he could still move us. "As the most avid curator of his own legend," he wasn't allowed to slip. He was reluctant to play in old-timers' games, "because he didn't want to disappoint."

"As explosive as his early fame was," he never did disappoint us as a player. Nor did he disappoint his teammates. "He helped make them winners," whereas the Yankees of the twenty-first century have yet to find another Jolter. "A-Rod doesn't help you [as much as DiMaggio did]," Bob said about Alex Rodriguez, the Yankee star third baseman and home run king.

"The modern ballplayer emerges with DiMaggio—he's historical. He marked his era" in a way that A-Rod never will. Like A-Rod, the Jolter was the highest-paid player of his time. But A-Rod never played in such constant pain. Bone spurs haunted the last half of DiMaggio's career. Yet we grew to love his tortured ballet; he could still beat young Mickey Mantle to a fly ball in his own vast territory of center field. No other player ever filled us with such a sense of the *unknown*. If he continues to bother our psyche, it's because no one has ever really replaced him. He wouldn't move to first base, as Mantle did, and fumble around like some half-man. Crippled as he was, the Jolter had the stride of a wounded wolf. We never doubted his devotion. Broken down or not, "DiMaggio was doing his very best for us. Mantle wasn't, and Williams was only doing his half-best for us," recalls Lipsyte.

"The world changed around him." Lipsyte remembers "the terrible shit he took when he held out briefly" before the start of the 1938 season. The fans, who had loved him in '37, turned against their darling. It took him weeks to woo them back. And it only added to his suspicious nature. He'd fought with the Yankees over a few miserable thousand dollars and had to give in. "He never made the kind of money he would have made" had he patrolled center field ten or twenty years later. "He was getting a lot of crap" for his Mr. Coffee commercials, while players' salaries began to jump over the moon. "He lived into another generation, saw what everybody else was doing," and it filled him with rage.

In his own lifetime, baseball had gone from a sport—with teams of nine men toiling on a lonely field—to a carnival show where players are "an extension of the entertainment industry."

And what a price we've had to pay, as all of baseball has become a band of greedy Methuselahs who want to remain on the field forever with their pumped-up bodies while they collect fatter and fatter checks. Harvey Araton of the *New York Times* believes that Barry Bonds and Mark McGwire and the other "juicers" "were only symptoms of an insidious culture," a culture of want that was willing to forgive any abuse, any infraction, if only McGwire or Sammy Sosa would hit another *Ruthian* home run. But McGwire and Sosa and Bonds were not Yankees, not members of that elite club. It took the Mitchell Report, released on December 13, 2007, and its investigation into the rampant use of steroids in the major leagues to out Roger Clemens, Andy Pettitte, Chuck Knoblauch, and eight other Yankees. And in 2009 *Sports Illustrated* revealed that A-Rod himself had tested positive for testosterone and anabolic steroids in 2003, while he was still a Texas Ranger.[14]

"I was young. I was stupid. I was naïve," A-Rod confessed to ESPN. It was all part of "the loosey-goosey era," when players thought they had an elixir that could make them immortal on the field. But there's no such elixir, and there never was, not even for A-Rod, who would help the 2009 Yankees win their first World Series in nine years.

Somehow, I can't imagine an infielder's or outfielder's sky for Rodriguez. The Yanks might have faltered as he missed the first part of 2009, but I never had the feeling that he was the team's essential glue. Perhaps no one can be in an age of multimillionaire players who are like Samurai warriors as they flit from team to team. A-Rod is articulate and affable—and a world away from the Jolter. It's hard to think of Joe DiMaggio ever confessing any kind of sin to ESPN. He would have been mortified. He had a mystery about him that none of the current Yankees will ever have. Yet there is a resemblance between A-Rod and the Jolter.

Like DiMaggio, he was born into an immigrant family of modest means. And like DiMaggio, he was a star at a very early age, winning the American League batting title when he was twenty-one. But he's still a Samurai, who gathered up his millions and moved from the Seattle Mariners to the Texas Rangers in 2001, and then to the Bombers in 2004. Perhaps the Jolter might have had the same wanderlust had there been no reserve clause in the 1940s. We'll never know.

A-Rod is my personal favorite among the latter-day Yanks, with his own brand of lightning and electricity at the plate. But he lacks the restlessness—the almost religious anticipation—that I remember from DiMaggio's days in the Bronx. DiMaggio was the only one who could silence an entire stadium. Perhaps we don't demand as much from A-Rod. Baseball was once our devotional, our secular church, and we expected *everything* from the Jolter. We felt his pain when he couldn't deliver, and his pain was ours.

5.

Baseball wasn't a huckster's paradise when the Jolter was in the middle of his streak. At least it wasn't for the players. One has to wonder what Kenesaw Mountain Landis and Happy Chandler, baseball's first two commissioners, might have thought of players growing magical mountains of muscle. We don't have to ponder about Bud Selig, baseball's current commissioner, a folksy and congenial man who would croon in 1995: "If baseball has a problem, I must say candidly that we were not aware of it," while the home run derbies of McGwire & Co. revived baseball's sagging attendance and brought the game roaring into a new century. If Selig shut his eyes, it was because Mark McGwire and Sammy Sosa (and later Alex Rodriguez) seemed good for business.[15]

And now, according to Murray Chass, baseball has its own "Hall of Infamy," whose charter members are Bonds, Clemens, McGwire, and Pete Rose. But it sounds a bit sanctimonious to crystallize baseball's affliction around a bunch of All-Stars. As Bruce Jenkins said in the *San Francisco Chronicle:* "Bonds was a steroid guy who came up to the plate against a steroid guy and grounded out to a steroid guy. Next time up, he got robbed on a great catch by a steroid guy. . . . Silence the moralists. It wasn't a pretty sight."[16]

A player's career, former outfielder Doug Glanville reminds us, "is always a blink in a stare." He arrives, becomes a wonder boy, then watches himself begin to wane as he runs from the nightmare of his own coming annihilation in the big leagues. "Enter steroids."[17]

It's an invidious ride, where players were "imbued with the belief that a failure to cheat and risk one's health was made at the potential cost of a career," writes Harvey Araton. One can only recall the Clipper, who couldn't thrive without his endless half-cups of coffee during a game, who had a terrifying need not to falter once, and who wouldn't let the Mick or any other Yankee outfielder intrude upon his domain; DiMaggio never would have danced with Morris Engelberg on a playing field. It's not that he was holier than Roger Clemens or A-Rod or Mark McGwire. It's that he would never have allowed himself to swell up in front of our eyes the way Bonds and McGwire did, and become a baseball Frankenstein.[18]

We remember him for the silver in his hair, for his demonized and masochistic devotion to Marilyn, for the childlike pride he had in his own game and the melancholy that seized him whenever he couldn't help the Yankees win, but most of all, we remember him as an icon that is embedded in the American dream. He was almost fictional, a kind of Jay Gatsby transposed from the Jazz Age to the Depression and the shock of wealth after World War II; like Gatsby, the Jolter arrived out of nowhere and had to invent himself; both of them believed in Scott Fitzgerald's orgiastic green light, in the notion of a magical, limitless future that seemed to rise right out of the "fresh, green breast of the new world," right out of the

American mist. And DiMaggio remains a distinctly American icon, one that could have been born in no other place, not only because baseball is *our* pastime but because the game itself was once linked with the nation's innocence and ambition.[19]

Fitzgerald's narrator, Nick Carraway, is startled when he meets Meyer Wolfsheim, the gambler who helped fix the World Series of 1919. "It never occurred to me," says Nick, "that one man could start to play with the faith of fifty million people—with the single-mindedness of a burglar blowing a safe."[20]

It's no accident that the Yankee dynasty, and its dominance through most of the twentieth century, began just after the Black Sox scandal, with the arrival of Ruth, then Gehrig, DiMaggio, Mantle, Yogi Berra, Whitey Ford, Roger Maris, Reggie Jackson, A-Rod, and Derek Jeter, like some phantasmagoric replica of American corporate life played out in pinstripes. Underlying this pinstripe army are the ghosts of Shoeless Joe Jackson and the other bumpkins who tossed away the World Series for peanuts and the promise of a gold mine. Jackson's fall from grace, his anonymous journey across America with his glove and bats, is a far cry from Clemens and McGwire withdrawing into their gated communities with a real gold mine. Jackson is as sad as history and myth. And the Jolter seems to share the same sadness and silence. He wasn't a country boy with paper clips in his pocket; he dressed like a movie star, but there's a curious string that ties DiMaggio with Shoeless Joe, a gorgeousness about their play that could only have happened at a time when baseball itself was a spectacle that had not yet morphed into a piece of the entertainment machine, but was rather like a wild country where entire teams could rush out onto the field for a battle royal, while their fans joined them or sat back in ribald delight.

Players and fans were barnstormers in their own fashion, with each year a constant, glorious summer, so that DiMaggio could sit in San Francisco or forage through the streets of Manhattan in a snowstorm and still feel he was five minutes away from center field. There was always "an outfielder's sky" for the Jolter, no matter where he was. That sky was the mark of his own myth; he and Shoeless Joe had very little lore outside of baseball itself. Their culture was the culture of the game. The Jolter didn't have a magic bat, like Black Betsy, or a glove held together with paper clips. But he had his sweet spot in center field. And he couldn't woo Marilyn with anything other than the grace he'd had on the field, or offer her much besides the devotion of an ex-outfielder whose insights were limited to an outfielder's sky.

He was her Slugger and would remain so, even when she was married to her Owl. It was a twentieth-century romance, foolish and full of heartbreak, and we remember the way he mourned her while he unraveled. He was a proletarian prince, wounded in one heel; it wasn't any of his records—his MVPs, his batting championships, his destruction of the Red Sox during the 1949 pennant race, even his hitting streak in '41—that sticks to us as much as the memory of that heel. He was our Philoctetes, wrenched from Greek myth, who could redeem us through his suffering. In his last four years as a major leaguer, he seldom played without a good deal of pain. We could see him grimace under the pinched bill of his baseball cap, watch him limp after a devilish tear into second base. We worried that he might not rise up again in that special shoe of his, his cleatless cleat. And when he did retire in '51, weren't we a little relieved that at least now he wouldn't be crippled for life? But we haven't stopping dreaming of him and the outfielder's sky that only he could reveal . . .

The only other athlete who ever haunted me as much as Di-Maggio was Bill Russell of the Boston Celtics. Russell was like a tall octopus with two arms rather than eight; but he might as well have had eight arms out on the court. He could block any ball with those tentacles of his. But there was never an extra motion or an extra move. He would glide past an opponent like an elegant ghost and close off every avenue to the basket. Russell's cool fire reached beyond basketball. He had a kind of poetry that no one else on the court understood or possessed. That didn't remove him from his teammates. He was the ultimate team player. But none of the other Celtics could approach his strange syncopation.

DiMaggio also had a language of his own. It wasn't simply that he was all by himself in center field, a wayfarer a world from home plate. The whole team moved according to his rhythm, depended on it, but could never really grasp the undercurrents of that rhythm. No one could. The Yankee Clipper was a singularity, a freak of nature who emerged out of nowhere with a sense of form. He was moody, inarticulate without his bat and glove. But until that heel hobbled him, his play was like a string of perfect sentences. And I realized that DiMaggio, who could barely pronounce his name in public, was a novelist's dream. The phantom that Grantland Rice wrote about in "An Ode to the Jolter" was as much of an artist as an athlete. His outfielder's sky wasn't inhabited by any other player; it was that kingdom where he thrived. And those of us who ever watched him could feel a melody that was akin to baseball but wasn't really a part of it.

In *Lives Like Loaded Guns,* Lyndall Gordon writes that Emily Dickinson's celebrated dashes, which allowed her to catapult the reader from image to image without a chance to breathe, "push the language apart to open up the space where we live without language." But that space without language is also a language. And it's into this territory that DiMaggio takes us, an incredible chasm where no one else has ever dared to go.[21]

Notes

Prologue

1. Simons, "Joe DiMaggio and the American Ideal," 21.
2. Grantland Rice, "An Ode to the Jolter," *Sporting News*, 1947; 66; Cramer, "What Do You Think of Ted Williams Now?" 66.
3. Cramer, *Joe DiMaggio*, xi.
4. Cramer, "What Do You Think of Ted Williams Now?" 126.
5. Cramer, *Joe DiMaggio*, 479.
6. DiMaggio, *Lucky to Be A Yankee*, 52; Allen, *Where Have You Gone, Joe DiMaggio?* 177.
7. Allen, *Where Have You Gone, Joe DiMaggio?* 151.
8. Updike, "Hub Fans Bid Kid Adieu," 305.
9. Quoted in Allen, *Where Have You Gone, Joe DiMaggio?* 64, 58; Halberstam, *Summer of '49*, 62.
10. Halberstam, *Summer of '49*, 60; Talese, "The Silent Season of a Hero," 4; Vecsey, "DiMaggio Left a Mark."
11. Allen, *Where Have You Gone, Joe DiMaggio?* 99, 87.
12. Cramer, *Joe DiMaggio*, 113.
13. Mailer, *Marilyn*, 97.
14. Cramer, *Joe DiMaggio*, 327.
15. Spoto, *Marilyn Monroe*, 325.
16. Mailer, *Marilyn*, 100.

17. Allen, *Where Have You Gone, Joe DiMaggio?* 160; Cramer, *Joe DiMaggio*, 331.

18. Jacobson, *Toots;* Bainbridge, "Toots World: I, How Far Can We Go?" 50.

19. Bainbridge, "Toots World: I, How Far Can We Go?" 72.

20. Ibid.

21. Bainbridge, "Toots World: I, How Far Can We Go?" 50; Bainbridge, "Toots World: II, Friendship," 56.

22. Bainbridge, "Toots World: II, Friendship," 56.

23. Brainbridge, "Toots World: III, Guys Like Us," 73.

ONE
"Our National Exaggeration"

1. Creamer, *Babe*, 154.

2. Ibid., 221, 14, 191.

3. Ibid., 330.

4. Burns and Sanders, *New York*, 360.

5. Smith, "The Babe Was Always a Boy," 161; Creamer, *Babe*, 321.

6. Creamer, *Babe*, 318, 81.

7. Ibid., 403.

8. Ibid., 403; Schumach, "Babe Ruth, Baseball Idol."

9. Creamer, *Babe*, 428.

10. Burns and Sanders, *New York*, 315, 317; Leach, "Brokers and the New Corporate, Industrial Order," 235.

11. Burns and Sanders, *New York*, 360.

12. Douglas, *Terrible Honesty*, 64; Creamer, *Babe*, 322; Berra, Introduction to *Sultans of Swat*, 59.

TWO
The Walloping Wop

1. Allen, *Where Have You Gone, Joe DiMaggio?* 17.

2. Cramer, "What Do You Think of Ted Williams Now?" 74.

3. Allen, *Where Have You Gone, Joe DiMaggio?*, 51.

4. Cramer, "What Do You Think of Ted Williams Now?" 74.

5. Simon, "The Silent Superstar," 2.

6. Simons, "Joe DiMaggio and the American Ideal," 37.

7. Cramer, "What Do You Think of Ted Williams Now?" 164, 63.

8. Allen, *Where Have You Gone, Joe DiMaggio?* 55.

9. Engelberg and Schneider, *DiMaggio*, 30.

10. Halberstam, *Summer of '49*, 56; Engelberg and Schneider. *DiMaggio*, 287.
11. Allen, *Where Have You Gone, Joe DiMaggio?* 74.
12. Gould, "The Streaks of Streaks," 174, 175.
13. Ibid.," 185.
14. DiMaggio, *Lucky to Be a Yankee*, 207.
15. Gould, "The Streaks of Streaks," 187.
16. Seidel, *Streak*, xi.
17. Ibid., xii, 1.
18. Ibid., 1.
19. Ibid., 5, 16.
20. Ibid., xiii.
21. Ibid., 225.
22. Ibid., 223.
23. Ibid., 2, 3.

THREE

Joltin' Joe and the Ghost of Lou Gehrig

1. Seidel, *Streak*, 11; 93.
2. Cramer, *Joe DiMaggio*, 192; Allen, *Where Have You Gone, Joe DiMaggio?* 85.
3. Eig, *Luckiest Man*, 207, 205.
4. Ibid., 360.
5. Cramer, "What Do You Think of Ted Williams Now?" 74.
6. Cramer, *Joe DiMaggio*, 198.
7. Cramer, "What Do You Think of Ted Williams Now?" 74.
8. Cramer, *Joe DiMaggio*, 210.

FOUR

"C'mon, Joe, Talk to Me"

1. Pennington, "The Forgotten Pioneers."
2. Berkow, "17 from Black Baseball."
3. Brashler, *Josh Gibson*, 24–25.
4. Ibid., 42, 40.
5. Ibid., 142, 129, 130.
6. Ibid., 137, 136.
7. Buck O'Neil, quoted in Berkow, "17 from Black Baseball."
8. Creamer, *Babe*, 41, 185, 270.
9. Brashler, *Josh Gibson*, 142.
10. Eig, *Luckiest Man*, 2.

11. Eig, *Opening Day*, 12.
12. Eig, *Luckiest Man*, 23, 4, 44.
13. Engelberg and Schneider, *DiMaggio*, 99.
14. Cramer, *Joe DiMaggio*, 226.
15. Allen, *Where Have You Gone, Joe DiMaggio?* 41.
16. Cramer, *Joe DiMaggio*, 236.
17. Ibid., 315; Allen, *Where Have You Gone, Joe DiMaggio?* 93.
18. Halberstam, *Summer of '49*, 206.
19. Ibid., 207.

FIVE
The Wounded Warrior

1. DiMaggio, *Lucky to Be a Yankee*, 137.
2. Cramer, *Joe DiMaggio*, 256.
3. Ibid., 251.
4. Allen, *Where Have You Gone, Joe DiMaggio?* 91.
5. Creamer, *Babe*, 403.
6. Helfers and Davis, "The DiMaggio Era," 78.
7. Allen, *Where Have You Gone, Joe DiMaggio?* 21–23.
8. Cramer, *Joe DiMaggio*, 261.
9. Allen, *Where Have You Gone, Joe DiMaggio?* 101.
10. Ibid., 106, 105.
11. Durso, "Joe DiMaggio"; Allen, *Where Have You Gone, Joe DiMaggio?* 69.
12. Allen, *Where Have You Gone, Joe DiMaggio?* 100, 127.
13. Cramer, *Joe DiMaggio*, 306, 303.
14. Allen, *Where Have You Gone, Joe DiMaggio?* 122; Cramer, *Joe DiMaggio*, 297, 300.
15. Allen, *Where Have You Gone, Joe DiMaggio?* 121.
16. Cramer, *Joe DiMaggio*, 313.
17. Allen, *Where Have You Gone, Joe DiMaggio?* 128.
18. Halberstam, *Summer of '49*, 46.

SIX
The Princess of Yankee Stadium

1. Halberstam, *Summer of '49*, 5, 137.
2. Cramer, *Joe DiMaggio*, 315.
3. Mailer, *Marilyn*, 118.
4. Ibid., 78.

5. Cramer, *Joe DiMaggio*, 324.
6. Mailer, *Marilyn*, 157.
7. Ibid., 97.
8. Leaming, *Marilyn Monroe*, 34; Kazan, *A Life*, 408, 540, 415.
9. Kazan, *A Life*, 455.
10. Mailer, *Marilyn*, 96.
11. Cramer, *Joe DiMaggio*, 333.
12. Allen, *Where Have You Gone, Joe DiMaggio?* 139.
13. Cramer, *Joe DiMaggio*, 329; 331; Leaming, *Marilyn Monroe*, 86.
14. Mailer, *Marilyn*, 119.

SEVEN
Mr. Marilyn Monroe

1. Allen, *Where Have You Gone, Joe DiMaggio?* 143.
2. Spoto, *Marilyn Monroe*, 325.
3. Cramer, *Joe DiMaggio*, 357.
4. Ibid., 360.
5. Mailer, *Marilyn*, 118; Spoto, *Marilyn Monroe*, 329.
6. Spoto, *Marilyn Monroe*, 339.
7. Cramer, *Joe DiMaggio*, 362.
8. Churchwell, *Many Lives of Marilyn Monroe*, 233.
9. Ibid., 363.
10. Ibid., 366.
11. Allen, *Where Have You Gone, Joe DiMaggio?* 144.
12. Leaming, *Marilyn Monroe*, 127.
13. Spoto, *Marilyn Monroe*, 349.
14. Cramer, *Joe DiMaggio*, 367; Spoto, *Marilyn Monroe*, 350.
15. Cramer, *Joe DiMaggio*, 368.
16. Ibid., 370.

EIGHT
"Bigger Than the Statue of Liberty"

1. Allen, *Where Have You Gone, Joe DiMaggio?* 148.
2. Ibid., 149.
3. Leaming, *Marilyn Monroe*, 135.
4. Capote, *Music for Chameleons*, 230.
5. Leaming, *Marilyn Monroe*, 168.
6. Miller, *Timebends*, 359.

7. Leaming, *Marilyn Monroe*, 174.

8. Allen, *Where Have You Gone, Joe DiMaggio?* 158.

9. Ibid., 158; Churchwell, *Many Lives of Marilyn Monroe*, 242.

10. Cramer, *Joe DiMaggio*, 376.

11. Liz Renay, *My First 2,000 Men* (Fort Lee, N.J.: Barricade, 1992), 379; Cramer, *Joe DiMaggio*, 379.

12. Cramer, *Joe DiMaggio*, 377.

13. Allen, *Where Have You Gone, Joe DiMaggio?* 156; Cramer, *Joe DiMaggio*, 384.

14. Allen, *Where Have You Gone, Joe DiMaggio?* 156.

15. Spoto, *Marilyn Monroe*, 455.

16. Ibid., 456.

17. Churchwell, *Many Lives of Marilyn Monroe*, 332.

18. Leaming, *Marilyn Monroe*, 306.

19. Cramer, *Joe DiMaggio*, 388.

20. Ibid., 386, 387.

21. Leaming, *Marilyn Monroe*, 304.

22. Ibid., 322; Crowe, *Conversations with Wilder*, 157.

23. Leaming, *Marilyn Monroe*, 371.

24. Cramer, *Joe DiMaggio*, 390.

25. Ibid., 394.

26. Ibid., 399, 401.

27. Ibid., 395.

28. Ibid., 410.

29. Ibid., 411.

30. Allen, *Where Have You Gone, Joe DiMaggio?* 157.

31. Cramer, *Joe DiMaggio*, 414.

32. Allen, *Where Have You Gone, Joe DiMaggio?* 157.

33. Simon, "The Silent Superstar," 2; Miller, *Timebends*, 436, 532; Leaming, *Marilyn Monroe*, 410.

34. "Brilliant Stardom and Personal Tragedy."

35. Churchwell, *Many Lives of Marilyn Monroe*, 312.

36. Wolfe, *The Assassination of Marilyn Monroe*, 412.

37. Spoto, *Marilyn Monroe*, 534.

NINE

The Greatest Living Ballplayer

1. Talese, "The Silent Season of a Hero," 16.

2. Ibid., 7.

3. Engelberg and Schneider, *DiMaggio*, 76.
4. Talese, "The Silent Season of a Hero," 14.
5. Engelberg and Schneider, *DiMaggio*, 70; Simon, "The Silent Superstar," 2.

TEN

The Biggest Fan of Them All

1. Engelberg and Schneider, *DiMaggio*, 106.
2. Ibid., 107, 127.
3. Ibid., 153.
4. Ibid., 119.
5. Ibid., 137, 127, 346.
6. Ibid., 122.
7. Ibid., 1.
8. Ibid., 108, 284; Castro, *Mickey Mantle*, 238.
9. Engelberg and Schneider, *DiMaggio*, 384.
10. Ibid., 97.
11. Ibid., 203.
12. Ibid., 27, 28.
13. Borowitz, "The Lost Poems of Joe DiMaggio."
14. Zezima, "A Recluse?"; Boylan, "Raise High the P.R. Blitz."

Finale

1. Cramer, *Joe DiMaggio*, 124.
2. Ibid.
3. Castro, *Mickey Mantle*, 114.
4. Ibid., 115.
5. Ibid., 113.
6. Ibid., xi, 5.
7. Ibid., xiv; Engelberg and Schneider, *DiMaggio*, 64.
8. Castro, *Mickey Mantle*, 175, 236.
9. Ibid., 220.
10. Curry, "McGwire's Path Could Predict Bonds's."
11. Halberstam, *Summer of '49*, 165.
12. Cramer, *Joe DiMaggio*, 479.
13. Lipsyte interview.
14. Araton, "All-Juice Team."
15. Wilson and Schmidt, "Baseball Braces for Tough Report."
16. Chass, "Pettitte Plays a Pivotal Role"; Curry, "Election 2013."

17. Glanville, "In Baseball, Fear Bats."
18. Araton, "All-Juice Team."
19. Fitzgerald, *The Great Gatsby*, 182.
20. Ibid., 74.
21. Gordon, *Lives Like Loaded Guns*, 111.

Selected Bibliography

Allen, Maury. *Where Have You Gone, Joe DiMaggio?* New York: New American Library, 1975.

Araton, Harvey. "All-Juice Team Has Finally Found Its Ace: Clemens." *New York Times,* December 14, 2007.

Auker, Elden, and Tom Keegan. *Sleeper Cars and Flannel Uniforms: A Lifetime of Memories from Striking Out the Babe to Teeing It Up with the President.* Chicago: Triumph, 2006.

Bainbridge, John. "Toots World: I, How Far Can We Go?" *New Yorker,* November 11, 1950.

———. "Toots World: II, Friendship." *New Yorker,* November 18, 1950.

———. "Toots World: III, Guys Like Us Here Are Born to Have Fun." *New Yorker,* November 25, 1950.

Berkow, Ira. "17 from Black Baseball Included in Hall at Last." *New York Times,* July 30, 2006.

Berra, Yogi. Introduction to *Sultans of Swat: The Four Great Sluggers of the New York Yankees, as Originally Reported by the New York Times.* New York: St. Martin's Press, 2006.

Borowitz, Andy. "The Lost Poems of Joe DiMaggio." *New Yorker,* August 6, 2007.

Boylan, Jennifer Finney. "Raise High the P.R. Blitz." *New York Times,* February 1, 2010.

Brashler, William. *Josh Gibson: A Life in the Negro Leagues.* New York: Harper and Row, 1978.

"Brilliant Stardom and Personal Tragedy Punctuated the Life of Marilyn Monroe." *New York Times,* August 6, 1962.

Burns, Ric, and James Sanders. *New York: An Illustrated History.* New York: Knopf, 1999.

Capote, Truman. *Music for Chameleons.* 1980; rpt. London: Penguin Classics, 2000.

Castro, Tony. *Mickey Mantle: America's Prodigal Son.* Washington, D.C.: Potomac, 2002.

Charyn, Jerome. *Marilyn: La dernière déesse.* Trans. Geneviève Thomas. Paris: Gallimard, 2007.

Chass, Murray. "Pettitte Plays a Pivotal Role for Clemens." *New York Times,* January 9, 2008.

Churchwell, Sarah. *The Many Lives of Marilyn Monroe.* New York: Picador, 2005.

Cramer, Richard Ben. *Joe DiMaggio: The Hero's Life.* New York: Touchstone, 2001.

———. "What Do You Think of Ted Williams Now?" In Halberstam and Stout. *Best American Sports Writing.*

Creamer, Robert W. *Babe: The Legend Comes to Life.* New York: Simon and Schuster, 1974.

Crowe, Cameron. *Conversations with Wilder.* New York: Knopf, 1999.

Crowther, Bosley. " 'Pride of the Yankees,' a Film Biography of Lou Gehrig, with Gary Cooper and Teresa Wright, on View at Astor." *New York Times,* July 16, 1942.

Curry, Jack. "Election 2013 (or Later): Debates Already in Swing." *New York Times*, December 16, 2007.

———. "McGwire's Path Could Predict Bonds's." *New York Times*, July 23, 2006.

DiMaggio, Joe. *Lucky to Be a Yankee.* 1949; rpt. New York: Grosset and Dunlap, 1957.

Douglas, Anne. *Terrible Honesty: Mongrel Manhattan in the 1920s.* New York: Farrar, Straus and Giroux, 1995.

Durso, Joseph. "Joe DiMaggio, Yankee Clipper, Dies at 84." *New York Times*, March 9, 1999.

Eig, Jonathan. *Luckiest Man: The Life and Death of Lou Gehrig.* New York: Simon and Schuster, 2005.

———. *Opening Day.* New York: Simon and Schuster, 2007.

Engelberg, Morris, and Marv Schneider. *DiMaggio: Setting the Record Straight.* St. Paul: MBI, 2003.

Fitzgerald, F. Scott. *The Great Gatsby.* New York: Charles Scribner's Sons, 1925.

Frommer, Harvey. *A Yankee Century.* New York: Berkley, 2007.

Gilliam, Richard, ed. *Joltin' Joe DiMaggio.* New York: Carroll and Graf, 1999.

Glanville, Doug. "In Baseball, Fear Bats at the Top of the Order." *New York Times*, January 16, 2008.

Gordon, Lyndall. *Lives Like Loaded Guns: Emily Dickinson and Her Family's Feuds.* New York: Viking, 2010.

Gould, Stephen Jay. "The Streak of Streaks." In *Triumph and Tragedy in Mudville: A Lifelong Passion for Baseball.* New York: Norton, 2004.

Greenberg, Hank, with Ira Berkow. *Hank Greenberg: The Story of My Life.* 1989; rpt. Chicago: Triumph, 2001.

Haberman, Clyde. "Hard to Figure: The Drab Legacy of Jottin' Joe." *New York Times*, July 17, 2007.

Halberstam, David. *Summer of '49.* 1989; rpt. New York: Harper Perennial, 2006.

Halberstam, David, and Glenn Stout, eds. *The Best American Sports Writing of the Century.* New York: Houghton Mifflin, 1999.

Helfers, John, and Russell Davis. "The DiMaggio Era: Baseball from 1936–1951." In Gilliam, *Joltin' Joe DiMaggio.*

Hersh, Seymour M. *The Dark Side of Camelot.* Boston: Back Bay, 1998.

Jacobson, Kristi, director. *Toots: His Town. His Saloon.* DVD. New York: IndiePix Films, 2007.

Kazan, Elia. *A Life.* New York: Knopf, 1988.

Kempner, Aviva, director. *The Life and Times of Hank Greenberg.* DVD. Los Angeles: Twentieth Century–Fox, 2001.

Leach, William. "Brokers and the New Corporate, Industrial Order." In Taylor, *Inventing Times Square.*

Leaming, Barbara. *Marilyn Monroe.* New York: Crown, 1988.

Lipsyte, Robert. Interview with the author. December 2007.

Mailer, Norman. *Marilyn.* New York: Grosset and Dunlap, 1973.

Miller, Arthur. *Timebends: A Life.* New York: Grove, 1987.

Monroe, Marilyn. *Fragments: Poems, Intimate Notes, Letters.* Ed. Stanley Buchthal and Bernard Comment. New York: Farrar, Straus and Giroux, 2010.

Monroe, Marilyn, and Ben Hecht. *My Story.* Lanham, Md.: Taylor Trade, 2007.

Oates, Joyce Carol. *Blonde.* 2000; rpt. New York: Ecco, 2009.

Pennington, Bill. "The Forgotten Pioneers." *New York Times,* July 27, 2006.

Sandomir, Richard. "The Detailed Life of Joe DiMaggio, Minus Some of the Juicy Details." *New York Times,* July 16, 2007.

Schumach, Murray. "Babe Ruth, Baseball Idol, Dies at 53 After Lingering Illness." *New York Times,* August 17, 1948.

Seidel, Michael. *Streak: Joe DiMaggio and the Summer of '41.* 1988; rpt. Lincoln: University of Nebraska Press, 2002.

Simon, Paul "The Silent Superstar." In Gilliam, *Joltin' Joe DiMaggio.*

Simons, William. "Joe DiMaggio and the American Ideal." In Gilliam, *Joltin' Joe DiMaggio.*

Smith, Red. "The Babe Was Always a Boy—One of a Kind." In Halberstam and Stout, *Best American Sports Writing.*

Spoto, Donald. *Marilyn Monroe.* New York: Harper Paperbacks, 1994.

Talese, Gay. "The Silent Season of a Hero." In Halberstam and Stout, *Best American Sports Writing.*

Taylor, William R., ed. *Inventing Times Square.* New York: Russell Sage Foundation, 1991.

Updike, John. "Hub Fans Bid Kid Adieu." In Halberstam and Stout, *Best American Sports Writing.*

Vecsey, George. "DiMaggio Left a Mark in the Sands," *New York Times,* March 9, 1999.

———. "For Two, a Day of Recognition; For One, a Day of Reckoning." *New York Times,* January 10, 2007.

Wilson, Duff, and Michael S. Schmidt. "Baseball Braces for Tough Report from Mitchell." *New York Times,* December 13, 2007.

Wolfe, Donald H. *The Assassination of Marilyn Monroe.* New York: William Morrow, 1998.

Zezima, Katie. "A Recluse? Well, Not to His Neighbors." *New York Times,* February 1, 2010.

Index